# Program Design and Construction

**Prentice-Hall Series in Personal Computing**
Portia Isaacson, *Editor*

HIGGINS *Program Design and Construction*

# Program Design and Construction

DAVID A. HIGGINS

*Langston-Kitch*
*Topeka, Kansas*

Prentice-Hall, Inc., Englewood Cliffs, New Jersey 07632

*Library of Congress Cataloging in Publication Data*

HIGGINS, DAVID A

Program design and construction.

(Prentice-Hall series in personal computing)

Bibliography: p.

1. Electronic digital computers—Programming.

I. Title. II. Series.

QA76.6.H528 1979 001.6'42 78-31097

ISBN 0-13-729525-1

Editorial/production supervision and interior design by Chris Moffa
Cover design by **Jayne Conte**
Manufacturing buyer: Gordon Osbourne



Printed in the United States of America

10 9 8 7 6 5 4

PRENTICE-HALL INTERNATIONAL, INC., *London*
PRENTICE-HALL OF AUSTRALIA PTY. LIMITED, *Sydney*
PRENTICE-HALL OF CANADA, LTD., *Toronto*
PRENTICE-HALL OF INDIA PRIVATE LIMITED, *New Delhi*
PRENTICE-HALL OF JAPAN, INC., *Tokyo*
PRENTICE-HALL OF SOUTHEAST ASIA PTE. LTD., *Singapore*
WHITEHALL BOOKS LIMITED, *Wellington, New Zealand*

# Contents

# Foreword

In the last few years, a great deal has been learned about the design and implementation of computer programs. Unfortunately, there have been very few good books translating these new ideas into a form that could be used by people just getting into programming.

Books like this one are desperately needed today--especially those which are aimed at beginning programmers, whether thay are hobbyists or professionals. While the cost of computer hardware continues to drop dramatically, the cost of software has not kept pace. The only way to change this disparity is by developing new and more reliable software design techniques, and then educating the people who need this knowledge.

Too many individuals today tend to confuse the act of coding a program with the concept of program design. The two are not the same, and must remain inseparable even on the smallest of programs. Fortunately, this book is primarily concerned with the latter of the two concepts, and also the more important: program design.

Dave Higgins and I have been working together for a number of years now, and I am still suprised at his insights into the design and development of logical program structures. Dave's approach, as you will see in this book, is a fresh and direct one aimed at providing the beginning programmer with the fundamental design tools and techniques required to produce "well structured" programs. As Dave points out, logical and structured design is not dependent upon the choice of the programming language. For this book, he has chosen to show examples which are coded in BASIC. However, the same approach holds whether the language is FORTRAN, Pascal, APL or (God forbid) RPG II.

When writing a book about programming, particularly one aimed at the users of very small machines, there is a very real danger that too much emphasis will be placed on program "tricks," cute and obscure techniques which produce obscure results. Experience has taught us that such emphasis invariably leads on to poor programming practices and poor program design. In the long run, it is far better to be obviously wrong than obscurely right: if you are obviously wrong, someone will probably tell you; if you are obscurely right you may never know that you are getting the right answers.

Much of the basic material presented in this book has been worked out over the last few years by literally thousands of commercial programmers throughout the world. The publication of books such as this one serve to bring the latest and best in software technology together with the latest hardware technology. I certainly hope you find this book as readable and useful as I did.

Ken Orr

# Preface

This is not just another book on computer programming. This is not a book that will present just the grammatical and syntactical rules of a particular computer language. There are already many good reference books available which address that topic. The scope of this book is much wider than just that, and its objectives are much higher. It is the intention of this book to detail a process by which correct, working computer programs can be created.

As the title suggests, this book is divided into two main parts. The first part of this book will not be concerned with any form-and-format aspects of any particular programming language. The primary focus will be on the tools and techniques which may be used to ascertain the structure of (analyze) a problem, and then to create (synthesize) a logical process which will solve it. This analysis/synthesis process we will call design.

The second part of the book is devoted to the techniques one may use to transform such a logical solution into a practical, physical realization which may be used in the real world; in other words, how to construct a program from the logical design. In the second section, we will be using examples of the language BASIC, since variants of this language are very widespread throughout the microcomputer family of machines.

This particular book is primarily aimed towards the user of a microcomputer system, whether a hobbyist who wants to play space war and lunar lander games, or a businessman who wants to run the receivables and payables for his small company. Although the book is directed specifically at these types of people, the methods introduced in this text are by no means trivial; they would be just as valuable to a professional programmer in a very large commercial data processing shop. The principles and techniques presented herein are applicable to work done on any kind of computer, regardless of whether it is a huge, multiprocessing system with a billion words of storage, a home microcomputer, or even a hand-held programmable calculator. The requirements of all of these machines are the same: to get the correct answers. That is primarily what this book is concerned with: getting the correct answers.

A book of this type has been a long time in coming. Previous books in this general area sought to teach potential programmers only the syntax and the grammar of a programming language. Very little, if any mention was made of how to actually design the program that was to be written. This approach to teaching people how to program is a lot like giving a person a foreign language dictionary and expecting them to be able to compose documents that read like Shakespeare.

In a very real sense, the computer programs that we ask people to compose must be infinitely more exact and refined than the language of Shakespeare. Collectively, computer programs must today handle billions of dollars, names, numbers, dates, and facts, and be able to keep them all correct. It seems strange that with all of the responsibilities that we give to computer programmers these days we aren't more concerned with whether or not these people know how to write correct, functional, verifiable, and maintainable programs.

As it is, most potential programmers in commercial shops are expected to learn the process of programming by osmosis; they are taught a language and then put into a room with some "veteran" programmers with the hope that something will rub off. Most of the time this does not work, and if it does work it takes a very long time for a new programmer to become very competent. The average hobby computerist or small businessman working with a microcomputer does not even have the advantage of having a so-called "expert" programmer around to help him get started. He must learn both the techniques for program design and coding from a manual intended only to present the specifics of code.

With the ever increasing number of computers and computer-like devices being introduced into our everyday lives, more and more people are going to be called on to have at least a rudimentary skill for writing programs, and writing them correctly. This book is presented to enable people to learn how to design and construct logically correct programs.

No matter whether you are a carpenter, a painter, a plumber or an electrician, having the correct tools to do a job is often more than half the battle. The same is true for the computer program designer. Having the correct tools will be crucial to the success or the failure of the job--in this case the production of a useful and working computer program.

However, unlike all of the carpenters, painters, plumbers and the electricians of the world, the computer programmers tools are not physical tools, which can be held in the hand and swung about in the air. They are rather logical tools: techniques, methods, and ways of conceptualization.

Although the idea of a logical tool may be a first hard to accept, their existence is not hard to demonstrate. Take for instance the old Roman numeral system of counting vs. the Arabic numeral system in use in most parts of the world today. If you have ever tried to do even the simplest of arithmetic operations using just Roman numerals, you know that they are exceedingly difficult to work with. For instance, consider the multiplication of two simple numbers, XXVII (27) and XIII (13):

```
     XXVII                              27
   x  XIII                            x 13
   --------                           -----
     XXVII          -or-                81
     XXVII                             27
     XXVII                            -----
  CCLXX                                351
  ----------
  CCC L I
```

Why then is it so hard to multiply two numbers using Roman numerals? Obviously, the problem is not with the logical operation itself; if we do the same problem with Arabic numerals we can compute the answer quite easily in just a few seconds. The difficulty must lie with the logical tools that are used to solve the problem. You can see that the development of modern mathematics would never have come about without the introduction of something like the Arabic numbering system. It isn't that calculus and other advanced mathematic operations are impossible using Roman numerals; they are. But we would be bogged down for years trying to solve even the most elementary of equations, simply because the logical tool that we try to use is inadequate for the job.

In much the same way, the development of reliable computer program design techniques depended upon the emergence of a tool to fit the job. In the past, most all of the methods used to design complex and exacting procedures were inadequate or inappropriate for the task. One classic case is the use of the "flowchart" in the design of computer programs.

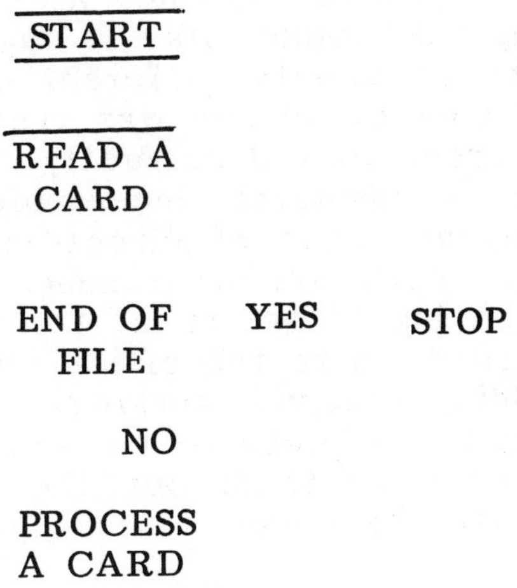

As their name implies, flowcharts map the flow of control for each individual step within a process. As clarification of this general flow, there is a different shape of box for every different type of step (process, decision, starting and stopping, etc.) that is represented. Each one of these boxes is connected to the others with an intricate pattern of directional arrows.

Flowcharts have been around in the computer industry for a long, long time, but their successes have been few and far between. They are relatively difficult to use from an intellectual standpoint and they are almost impossible to draw neatly. More often than not, large flowcharts end up being so huge and complex that they become nearly impossible for the human mind to comprehend. There is so much detail depicted that the overall process is lost: sort of a "can't find the forest for the trees" phenomenon.

Consequently, when pressed to use flowcharts to design programs, the programmers in commercial shops rebelled. Usually, they found it much easier to code "by the seat of their pants" and produce a flowchart after the fact (since they were required to do one). They would throw together a few lines of code into something that looked like it might work and then try it fifteen or twenty different times until it finally did. Of course, no one was ever absolutely sure that their program worked correctly because it had by this time become absolutely impossible to read. It had no structure, no sense of direction. That is why most commercial computer programmers have had the experience of having to get up at three o'clock in the morning to go down to the office and fix a program that has suddenly stopped working. Their programs were never really complete or correct, because they never would bother to think out the problem before they would write the code.

Tools are not very helpful if they are not used, and the flowchart, along with most of the other traditional techniques were never really widely used in design. But this book will present a new and much better tool than the tools of the past. It is a tool that is easy to learn and understand. It is a tool that is easy to get people to use. And it is a tool that has an undeniable selling point: it allows programmers to write correct programs that usually run on the very first try!

The tool is called Warnier-Orr diagramming. It represents one of the newest, state-of-the-art program design methods. It is a simple and yet very sophisticated and elegant technique which allows people to build programs better than ever before.

I think you will be pleased with this new tool.

D.A.H.

# Program Design and Construction

# 1

# Introduction to Computer Logic

## Computers

A few years ago, a breakthrough was made in the electronics industry which radically altered the process for the design and manufacture of computers and computer-like devices. It dramatically reduced the time, effort, and money required to produce a reliable computer. And as computer hardware became cheaper, smaller and easier to make, computers began to creep little by little into our daily lives: some cars now have miniature computer-like devices to regulate fuel consumption; microwave ovens have computer devices to control food processing; and the popular new home video games are controlled by true computers which would have been the size of a desk in the early 1960's. Computers have come out from behind the closed doors of the scientific and business communities and have moved into the home. This increasing visibility of the computer will continue at least through the end of the twentieth century.

This "computer age" began many years ago in America. The fondness of the American people for fancy gadgets like radios and later televisions insured a healthy climate for the growth and development of a healthy "gadget culture." By the 1960's, transistor radios that could be carried around in a shirt pocket were all the rage. Then, the gadget market shifted into high gear.

In the early 1970's, the first pocket calculators were marketed commercially. These marvelous (and incredibly expensive) little things could add, subtract, multiply, and divide with only the touch of a button. The public went crazy, and as more and more people bought them, their prices plummeted--units which had cost as much as four to five hundred dollars in 1971 were soon going for around thirty or forty dollars (a similar calculator today will cost about $9.95). Virtually anyone that wanted one could afford a pocket calculator.

Then, in 1975, a group of people in New Mexico announced and began advertising the first commercially available "microcomputer." It was a small but highly fuctional computer that cost less than an automobile. It wasn't really very useful, but it did spawn a new industry which grew very rapidly over the next few years.

Today, the microcomputers have advanced to the point that anyone with 600 dollars can walk into a neighborhood Radio Shack almost anywhere in the country and but one off of the shelf. Many other companies are offering similarly priced computers with comparable functions.

With this gradual onslaught of these new microcomputers, many people who had never even seen a computer before are discovering that they want or need to be able to communicate with them; they need to be able to instruct them to perform simple processes, such as keeping track of the company's accounts receivable or playing a Space War game. It is this art of instruction that is called computer programming. Computer programming is what this book is about.

## On Talking to a Computer

Computers cannot in any sense of the word be considered alive, so when we write of communication with a computer, we are using the word in a very loose manner. What we really mean by communication is the ability to instruct the computer to carry out certain tasks for us--long, complicated, or boring tasks that people are bad at and computers are good at.

Unfortunately, communication between computers and people is not nearly as easy as communication between people and other people. People can interpret what someone else has actually said into what they really meant to say. Even the biggest computers cannot do that.

For instance, if we were to ask a some other person to "Run down to the grocery store and pick up a loaf of bread, please," we could logically expect them to walk (or drive if it is very far) to the nearest grocery store, go in and buy a loaf of bread, and then bring it back. But they could only do that because they interpreted what was said into what was meant. Were they to have taken the words literally, as a computer would, they probably would have sprinted to the store, rushed in and lifted a loaf of bread high into the air. They would still be standing there too, since nothing at all was said about buying the loaf of bread or bringing it back.

Computers can do only and exactly what they are told to do: no more and no less. They aren't imaginative or interpretive. They can't go ahead and do something that someone has forgotten to them to do it. Computers are only as reliable as the people that have programmed them, and only as reasonable as the people who give them information.

It is obvious that if we want to have our computers behave in a predictable manner, we need to make sure that any sort of communication between ourselves and the computer is more highly refined and exact than simple everyday English. Typically, this communication will take the form of a list of elemental instructions, each one of which represents a simple action that the computer can perform. Taken together this list of elemental instructions comprises a task we want the machine to perform.

The degree of complexity of these elemental instructions varies with the particular programming language which is used; high level languages have statements that closely resemble English and are correspondingly easy for the programmer to use--low level languages manipulate the basic machine language instructions and require a great deal of knowledge about the actual internal workings of the computer. These lists of instructions then become a "recipe" which the computer will use to formulate a solution to the problem we have presented it with. This recipe we call a computer program.

Take the example that we used before of going to the store for a loaf of bread. Rather than being broad and imprecise about what exactly we want someone to do, we could give them a list of exact instructions to perform. The sentence "Run to the store and pick up a loaf of bread" would translate into a few simple instructions, put together to form a "psuedo-program." Such a list of instructions appears in Figure 1.1.

You could give someone this list and tell them to perform each step only once, starting at the top of the list and executing one step after another until they reach the end of the list. Then, even if someone did not know how to go to a store for bread, if they could understand and follow all of the instructions on the list they would eventually complete the task. This list is a very simple non-computer example of what a program might look like: a number of steps that are performed in sequential order.

It might seem from this example that compiling all of those simple actions together to form a more complex

Step 1. Walk to your car and get in.
Step 2. Start your car.
Step 3. Drive to the grocery store.
Step 4. Park your car.
Step 5. Shut off your car.
Step 6. Walk into the store.
Step 7. Find a loaf of bread.
Step 8. Pick up and hold the bread.
Step 9. Walk to the checkout counter.
Step 10. Pay for the bread.
Step 11. Walk out of store.
Step 12. Walk to your car and get in.
Step 13. Start your car.
Step 14. Drive back home.
Step 15. Park your car.
Step 16. Shut off car.
Step 17. Carry the loaf of bread inside.

Figure 1.1:
"How To Go To The Store To Buy A Loaf Of Bread"

act is a great deal of trouble and quite a complicated procedure. Fortunately in the long run, computer programming is not nearly as hard as it might seem from this first example. Of course, it takes a bit of skill and foresight to be able to list all of the necessary instructions in the proper order. In order to learn how to do that, we must first examine the problem, consider a solution, and only then assemble the list. We must first design the computer program before we can properly construct it.

## Program Design vs. Construction

No competent carpenter would seriously consider the prospect of building a three story townhouse without first having a blueprint to work from; likewise, no sensible electrician would try building a radio or television set without a schematic diagram. There are simply too many important things that might be left out by mistake or put together incorrectly.

In the same way, computer programmers who try to build programs by stringing lists of arbitrary instructions together to see if they will work generally do not have much success. Working from a plan that is thought out beforehand is a much more realistic approach. Ideally, what we as a programmer would like is some sort of a program "blueprint" that would indicate when, where, and how to put all of the program instructions together correctly. Therefore, before looking at the specifics of any particular programming language, we are first going to be concerned with the process of program design.

## Sets and Subsets

We will begin our discussion of program design with a brief plunge into an area which is at first glance unrelated to computer programming: the field of "set theory." In mathematics and elsewhere, you will run across the notion of a *set* and a *subset*. In program design, there is also a similar but slightly more restrictive concept of a set and a subset. In design, a set is said to be *an ordered collection of like objects* (objects that have some characteristic in common). A subset is simply a set within a set or, a little more formally, *an ordered collection of like objects that is wholly contained within some other set*. Sets in which all of the elements are contained in a larger set, but whose elements are in a different order, are not considered subsets.

Thus, if we wanted to build a set that contained all of the days of the week in order, it would look like this:

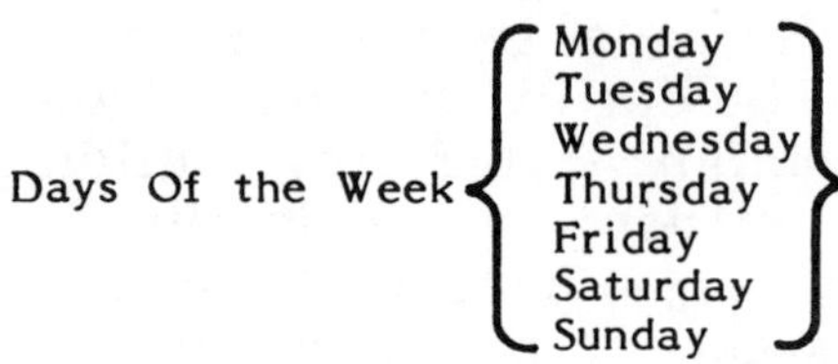


Figure 1.2: The Set Of Weekdays

This is set notation and you will find this the same as in mathematics. All of the *elements* of the set (each of the individual entries) are enclosed in braces, and the name of the set is written off to its left. A subset of this set might be

Days In A Weekend $\left\{ \begin{array}{l} \text{Saturday} \\ \text{Sunday} \end{array} \right\}$

Figure 1.3: A Weekday Subset -- The Weekend

Of course, this is not the only subset of the set of weekdays. Any ordered combination of days of the week would also be a subset; any set can have many different subsets.

If you go back and look closely at that list of instructions back in Figure 1.1, you should see that there are certain sets of instructions that the psuedo-program for going to the store could be broken up into--that is, certain groups of instructions which all run together to form a single task. The most obvious set we can see would include the entire list of instructions, and would be labeled "How to go to the store to get a loaf of bread." We could even draw it in traditional set notation. This way of representing the process appears in Figure 1.4.

Within this large set of instructions there are many smaller subsets of instructions that we can also identify. These subsets can all be considered to perform a single "sub-function" within the larger process. These will include such sets as: "Things to do to begin going to get a loaf of bread," which are instructions 1 and 2; "Things to do to drive the car to the store for a loaf of bread," which are instructions 3 through 14; and the "Things to do at the end of going to get a loaf of bread," which are instructions 15, 16 and 17. In set notation, those subsets could be drawn as in Figure 1.5.

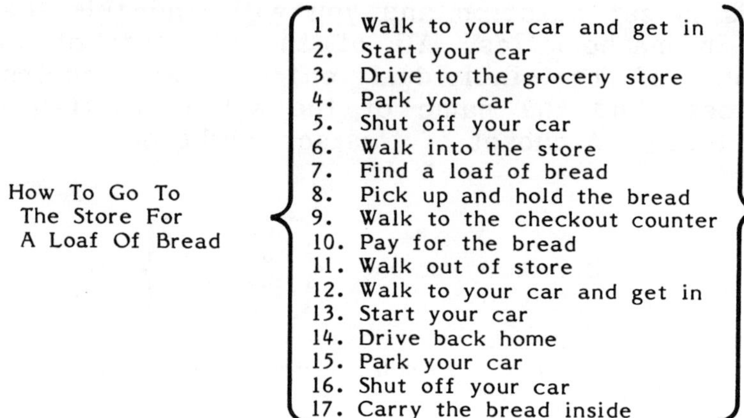


Figure 1.4: The Set "How To Go To The Store For A Loaf Of Bread"

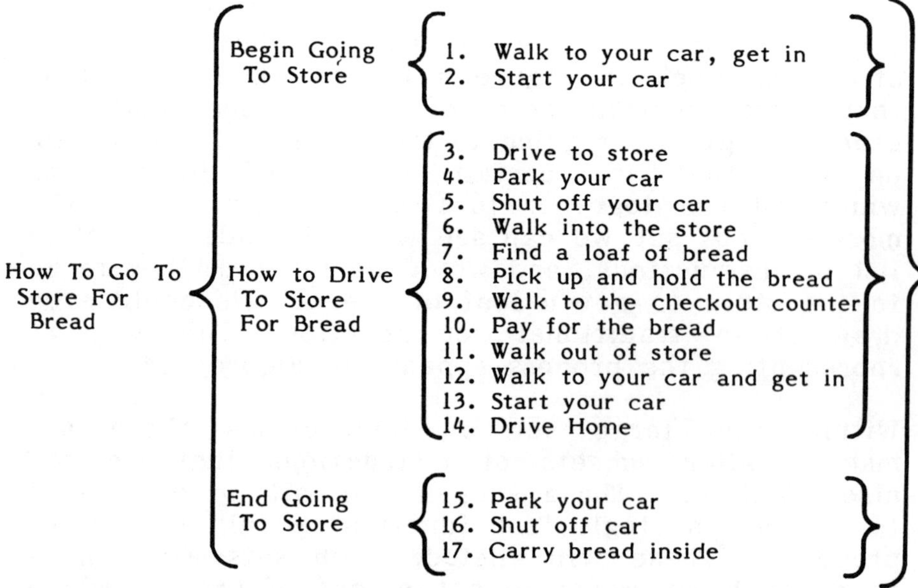


Figure 1.5: A Set With Subsets

But even the subset "How To Drive To Store For Bread" can be further broken down into still more subsets.

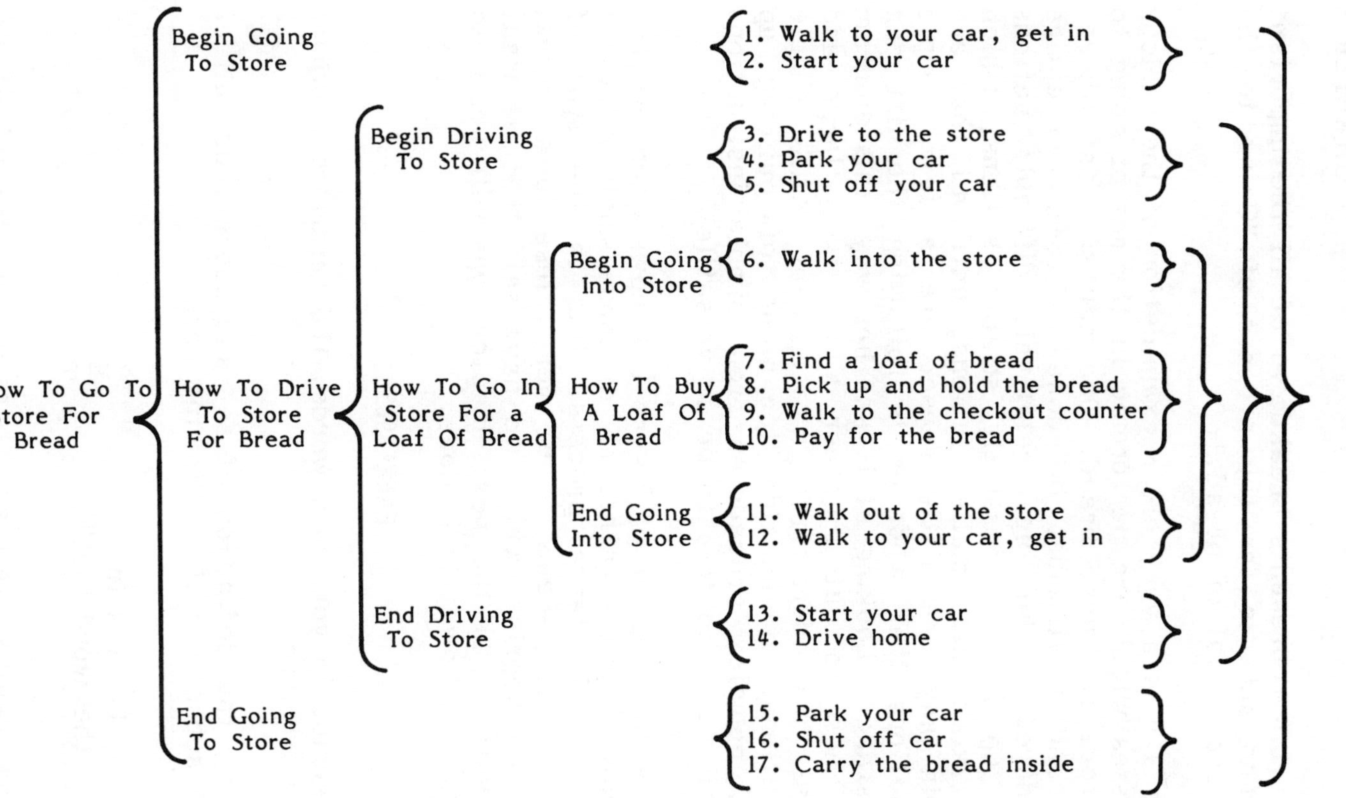


Figure 1.6: Getting Bread

Figure 1.6 represents breakdown of all the important sets and subsets for the process of "Going to the store for a loaf of bread."

Figure 1.6 is a very clear examination of the various processes which are performed in the act of going to the store for some bread. One can see just where, why, and what must be done to form the entire procedure. The big, relatively difficult actions break up into successively smaller actions, which break down into smaller actions, until all that are left in any one little subset are a few, simple instructions that whoever is following the list can understand. Looking at it another way, this diagram shows how to put together a relatively large and difficult procedure from a series of small, simple instructions. It is this technique of building up large, complex procedures from simple instructions that allows computers to be so versatile.

Because the diagram of Figure 1.6 shows when, where, and how to put together all of those small processes into a single large process, this is the type of diagram which seems to be very close to a logical program blueprint--which we have said that we want to develop. In the next chapter, we will begin to discuss just how this is done.

## EXERCISES

1. Describe in your own words, the terms *set*, *subset* and *program*.

2. Using the definition of set and subset, list all of the subsets in the following set:

| Letters in the word "set" | S<br>E<br>T |
|---|---|

2a. How many subsets are there of the ordered letters of the alphabet? What is the formula for computing the number of subsets of a set with "n" elements?

3. Order the following list of actions into sets and subsets following the example of Figure 1.6. The title of this set of actions is "How To Go Fishing."

1. Walk to car, get in
2. Start car
3. Drive car to lake
4. Park car
5. Shut off car
6. Walk to trunk of car
7. Get fishing pole and tackle box out of trunk
8. Walk to lake
9. Bait your hook
10. Cast line into lake
11. Wait for a fish to bite
12. Reel in fish
13. Unhook fish, put it on the stringer
14. Walk back to car
15. Put fishing supplies back in trunk
16. Get in car
17. Start car
18. Drive car home
19. Park car
20. Shut off car
21. Carry fish into house

4. Fill in the following sets and sub-sets of actions with the appropriate instructions that are given below.

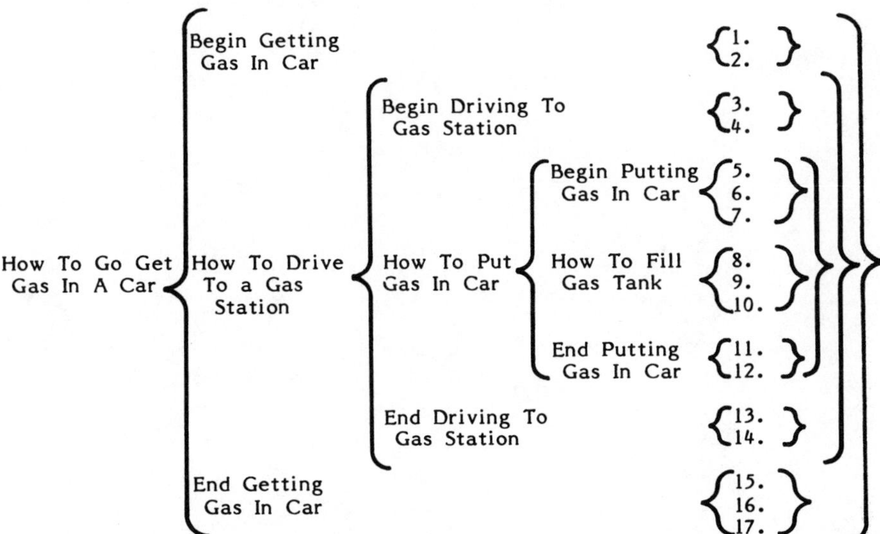

a. Shut off car
b. Take off gas cap
c. Pay for gas
d. Start car
e. Start car
f. Walk to gas tank
g. Walk into house
h. Drive home
i. When tank is full, stop filling
   tank and remove nozzle from tank
j. Insert nozzle into gas tank
k. Get back in car
l. Walk to car
m. Park car
n. Pull up to gas pump
o. Squeeze nozzle handle
p. Drive to gas station
q. Put gas cap back on

# 2

# Introduction to Warnier-Orr Diagrams

## Discovery in France

Our use of the set notation diagrams in Chapter 1 was a prelude of things to come. Such diagrams present the program lists in a very organized and easy to follow manner. This observation is not a new one. One of the first people to notice that set notation was extremely useful to break up process descriptions, was Jean-Dominique Warnier (pronounced warn-yay') of Paris, France. Back around the mid to late sixties, Warnier and his group of researchers developed a very sophisticated method of computer program design called "L.C.P.," which stands for "Logical Construction of Programs." They also began to use a sort of "set notation" diagram in their work. They called those charts that they made "lists of logical sequences," and used them to define and design detailed process descriptions which could be later turned into computer programs.

Warnier's ideas and theories were understandably slow in coming to the United States and even slower in being accepted, since most of his work was published in Paris and written in French. Their eventual acceptance in America is due in large part to the enthusiastic work of Kenneth T. Orr, who realized their significance and promoted them here in this country, while in turn developing further improvements to the basic diagrams which allowed them to become even more useful for computer program design. The work done by Orr and his group has resulted in a newer and better design technique based on the work of Warnier and others.

These Warnier-Orr diagrams, as they have come to be called in here in America, are gaining world-wide recognition as excellent systems analysis methods and reliable computer program design techniques. Although these techniques were originally developed for large commercial computers, the techniques and methods are just as valid for the smallest mini or microcomputer. And the rewards are just as gratifying.

### Warnier-Orr Diagrams

The basic form of the Warnier-Orr diagrams differs a bit from the set notation charts that were introduced in Chapter 1, but only by a minor technicality: the Warnier-Orr diagrams drop the right-hand brace that encloses each subset, since it is really unnecessary to the understanding of the logical groups described. The elimination of these redundant brackets makes the Warnier-Orr diagrams very simple without losing any of the great readability that the "set notation" charts had.

If we go back to to the last chapter for a moment and look at Figure 1.6, we find that we can represent that "set notation chart as a Warnier-Orr diagram. This diagram appears in Figure 2.1.

### Structured Processes

Warnier-Orr diagrams also have a few other functions that allow them to represent many more kinds of processes than just plain "set notation" diagrams will.

Two of the functional capabilities that they do share with the "set notation" diagrams are the ability to show the process of sequence and the concept of hierarchy. Sequence is the process of performing one action after another: first action #1, then #2, then #3,... and so on. We'll talk more about hierarchy in later chapters. It will suffice for now to say that hierarchy is the representation of the relationship between a set and one of its subsets.

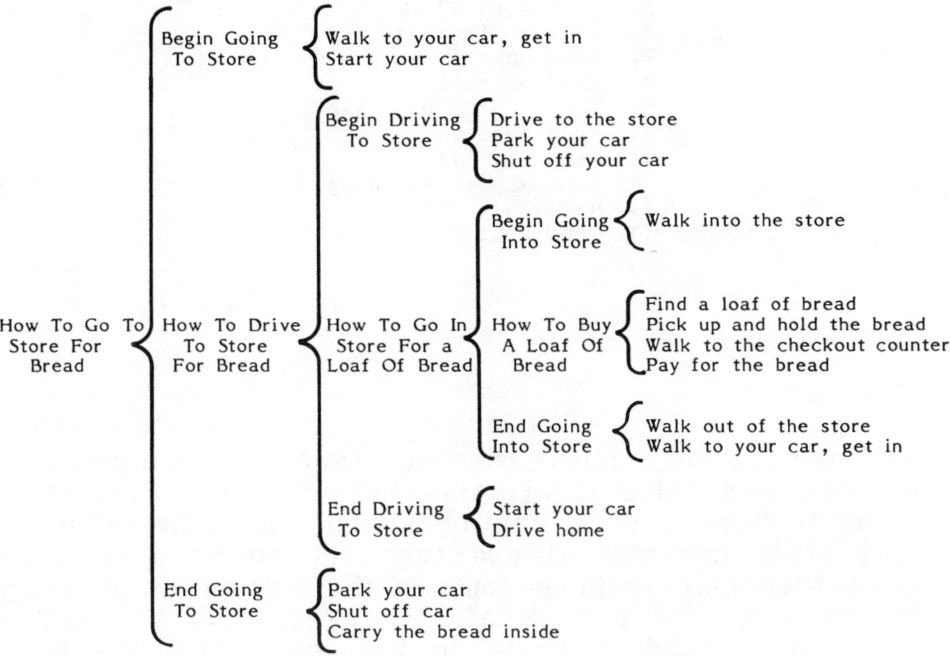


Figure 2.1: The Warnier-Orr Diagram

Two other processes that our set notation diagrams as given cannot represent are the processes of repetition and alternation, both of which are needed for process design. We shall examine the repetition function first.

## Repetition

If you wanted to be able to describe to a computer the exact process that a person might use to read a book, you could give it a list of instructions, such as those that appear in Figure 2.2.

1. Turn to page #1 of the book
2. Read page #1
3. Turn to the next page
4. Read page #2
5. Read page #3
6. Turn to the next page
7. Read page #4
8. Read page #5
9. Turn to the next page
10. Read page #6
11. Read page #7
12. Turn to the next page
13. Read Page #8
14. Read Page #9

.
.
.

Figure 2.2: How to Read a Book--Method 1

You can see that unless the book that you were going to read was quite short, this list of instructions is going to become very lengthy indeed. As a matter of fact, this list will always turn out to be a little more than half again as long as the number of pages in the book; for a book of 150 pages, say, the list required to read it would be 227 steps long! But if you look closely at the list in Figure 2.2, you can see that after the first two instructions, the next group of three instructions are repeated, with the only change between each group being that the page numbers that you are instructed to read are changed upwards each time. What we obviously need then is some way of being able to tell someone to "turn to the next page" and "read the left and right-hand pages" over and over again until all of the pages have been turned and read--to 'repeat' a given set of actions.

A Warnier-Orr diagram would represent that process like this:

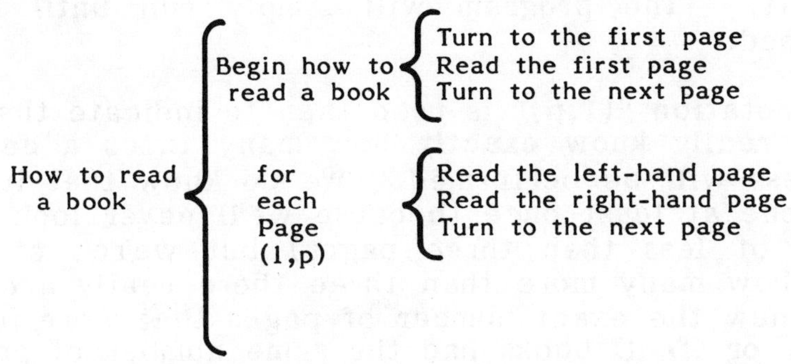


Figure 2.3: How to Read a Book--Method 2

The numbers in parentheses "(1,p)" beneath the process name "for each Page" indicate that this procedure is to be performed at least once and possibly a great number of times (indicated by a variable, in this case the letter "p" for "pages"). The "(1,p)" is read "one to 'p' times." Thus, for each page of the book, there is a defined set of actions to follow.

Notice that if we had wanted to use the list of instructions in Figure 2.2, we would have to know how many pages there were in a particular book beforehand, in order to include the proper number of "turn to the next page, read the left- and right-hand pages" instructions. This number would probably be very different for every book that we wanted to read, and we would have to change the length of our list of instructions each time in order to compensate.

If we had to program computers this way, we would have to change our program each time that we wanted to use it, which is very expensive and time consuming and obviously something that we'd like not to have to do. But with the use of the notation "(1,p)," we know to turn the pages of the book "until we are done," however many pages that turns out to be. This turns out to be ideal for computer programs, since we don't have to change a program each time we want to use it. The program will simply run until it is finished.

The notation "(1,p)" is used then to indicate that we don't really know exactly how many times a certain process will be performed. We do know that it will be done at least once (because we'll never look at a book of less than three pages) but we're not sure just how many more than three there really are. If we knew the exact number of pages that were in our book, or if all books had the same number of pages, we would not use the notation "(1,p)," we would instead write something like

Figure 2.4: For Books With 131 Pages

to indicate that the process is to be done an exact number of times. Of course, books don't all have exactly 131 pages, but there are many other things that we have to deal with in computer programming that do happen to occur in fixed numbers: for example, weeks always have seven days; years always have twelve months; and so on.

## Alternation

Although you've probably never thought about it, in the English language the word "or" has two different meanings. Up until now, that difference was sort of intuitive and unimportant. You probably even understood the difference between the two, even if you couldn't explain it.

For instance, if you were to tell someone that you had "a nickel or a quarter" in your pocket, and then it turned out that you had both, you wouldn't have lied: that statement was true. This is an example of an "inclusive OR" because it means "one or the other or both"; it 'includes' the case that both may be true.

If, however, you told someone that they could borrow your car on "Friday or Saturday night," and then they borrowed it both nights, you would probably be a little upset. What you meant, of course, is that they could have your car "either Friday or Saturday night but not both nights." This is the "exclusive OR," and unlike the inclusive OR, it is of great usage in the computer programming field. We will represent the "exclusive OR" on a Warnier-Orr diagram like this:

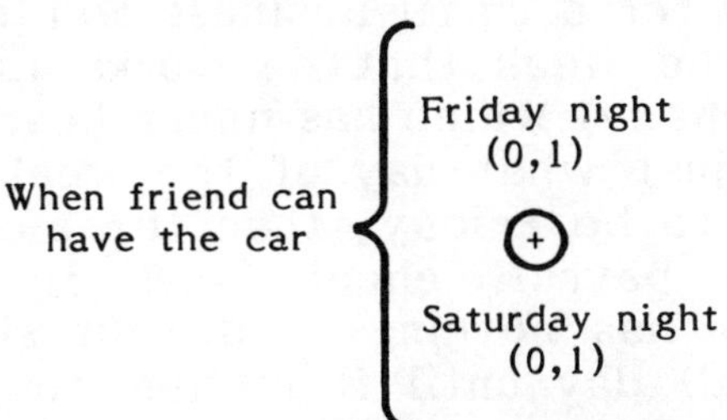


Figure 2.5: The "Exclusive OR"

The "⊕" is the symbol for the "exclusive OR" function, and it is used in conjunction with a 'number of times' notation of "(0,1)" beneath each process that it separates. Both processes are performed "zero or one times," since if my friend has the car the first night, then the process conditioned by "Friday night" is done once, and the process conditioned by "Saturday night" is not done at all. It is just the reverse if my friend has the car on the second night, so that both processes may occur "zero or one times," depending upon which condition is true.

This is called an alternative process structure. It says that one process or another will be performed, but both cannot be. An even more useful and probably a more common usage of the alternative structure is something called a 'complementary' situation and it looks like this:

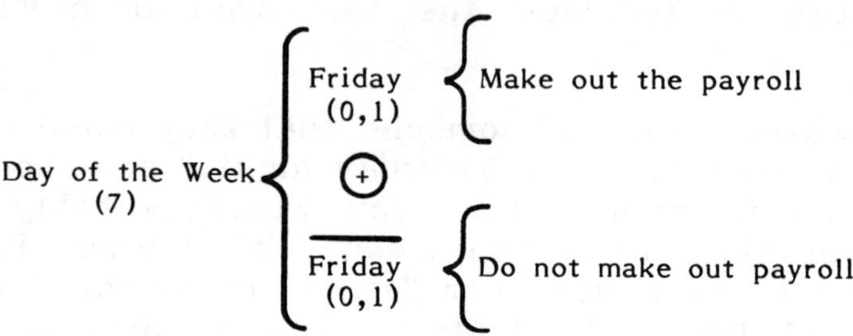


Figure 2.6: When to Make Out the Payroll

For this example, say that a clerk who makes out the payroll checks for a small business wants to know for each day of the week that he works (seven for this particular company, which has never heard of overtime or days off) just what day of the week it is. If the day turns out to be Friday, then the clerk must print up everyone's payroll check. If it isn't Friday, then the clerk has nothing to do but sit around and drink coffee all day until it is time to go home. On the Warnier-Orr diagram, the symbol '———' means the 'logical negation of', so that '$\overline{\text{Friday}}$' is read 'not Friday'. This is a complementary structure, since each condition is the logical complement of the other, and they describe every possible case (it either is Friday or it is not Friday, so that there is no other case to consider).

## The CASE Structure

There is another alternative structure that is often used extensively in process design, and it really amounts to no more than a generalized alternation, in which there are more than two cases to consider. It is called, suprisingly enough, a case statement, and is nothing more than three or more processes strung together in alternative fashion. It is used to select one path according to three or more possible conditions which may exist.

Say for instance, that we wanted to be able to do one of three different process depending on whether the day of the week was Monday, Wednesday, or Friday. We could do it with a case statement like this:

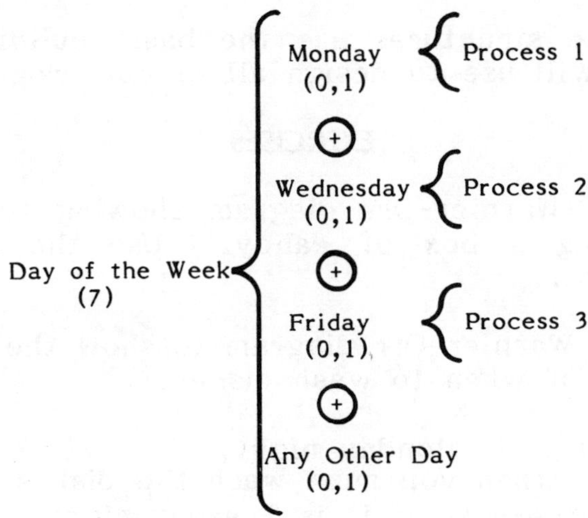


Figure 2.7: A CASE Statement

Notice that we included "Any Other Day" as one of the possible cases. Even if nothing is done when it isn't Monday, Wednesday, or Friday, the entry "Any Other Day" still has a logical place in the structure, since it completes the alternative complement. If there is really nothing at all to do for "Any Other Day," we would show that by writing the word "Skip" in it's bracket. It would then be called a 'null action', since, although it logically should appear on the diagram, nothing takes place there. This notation appears in Figure 2.8.

It has been known for many years that these three program structures--sequence, repetition, and alternation--are sufficient to build any program action.

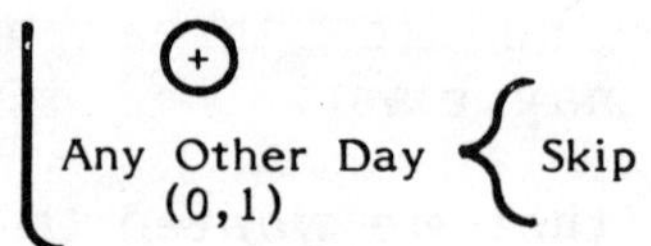


Figure 2.8: Null Action

These three structures are the basic building blocks which we will use to design all of our programs.

## EXERCISES

1. Draw a Warnier-Orr diagram showing the process of eating a box of candy. Use the repetitive structure.

2. Draw a Warnier-Orr diagram to show the following process of when to wash dishes.

   If it is Monday night,
      then you must wash the dishes
   otherwise if it is Tuesday night,
      then you must wash pots and pans
   otherwise,
      you must dry the dishes.

3. In the game of "BUG", two or more players take turns rolling a die, and each number on the die corresponds to a piece a BUG's body, detailed below:

| ROLL | | Part of BUG | Needed to finish BUG |
|---|---|---|---|
| 1 | = | Body | 1 |
| 2 | = | Neck | 1 |
| 3 | = | Head | 1 |
| 4 | = | Antennae | 2 |
| 5 | = | Tail | 1 |
| 6 | = | Leg | 6 |

The only other rules are as follows: you must have a body before you can have a neck, a tail or legs; you must have a neck before you can have a head; and you must have a head before you can have any antennae. The first player to complete a BUG wins the game.

Draw a Warnier-Orr diagram that details, for each roll of the die, the conditions that must be met in order to get that piece of the BUG.

For instance, if the player rolls a "1" on the die, the conditions look like this:

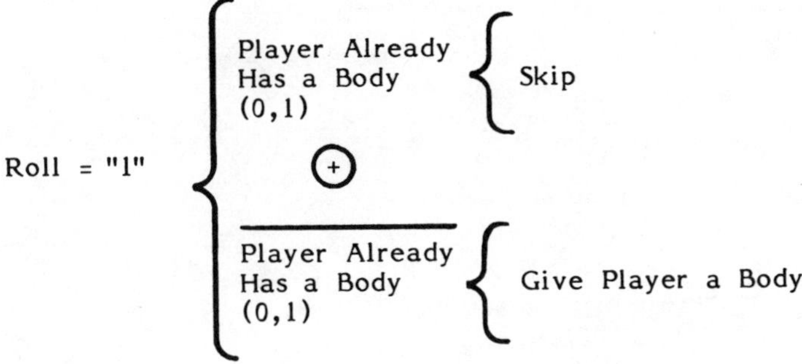

# 3

# Using Warnier-Orr Diagrams

## Structured Design

In the last chapter, we discussed the three basic building blocks used in the construction of the Warnier-Orr diagrams: the structures of sequence, repetition and alternation. Classically, these have been known as the structured processes used in structured design. Beginning with this chapter, we will start to be concerned with some of the ways that those small processes can fit together to form other, much larger processes and eventually, how they can be used to build correct computer programs.

Unlike a lot of other methodologies in use today, the Warnier-Orr techniques are based upon one very simple cardinal rule, a rule which will be followed each time that you design a process. And that rule is: you must design processes backwards!

That's right--backwards. Although it sounds impossible, designing backwards simply means that you don't start with the basic building blocks of the design technique and try to put them together to see what you can get. That is not the way to design anything! If you think about it, that is a lot like giving a carpenter a pile of bricks and boards and expecting him to put together a three story office building. It just dosn't work.

If however, an architect starts with the idea of a completed three story office building, and then goes about the process of 'taking it apart' mentally to find all of its basic components, he can then very easily tell a carpenter how to build it out of a pile of bricks and boards. This is what we mean by "designing backwards:" you start with the criterion of "knowing what you want when you are done", i. e., the envisioned final product, and then you break that finished product down into its basic building blocks. That is how you design processes also. You first design backward--you then construct forward.

### Designing Processes

Let's say that we want to design a process to describe to someone how to eat dinner at a restaurant. Since we must design backwards, we must by asking ourselves the question: what do we want to have when we are finished? Well, we know that what we want to have when we are done with this particular job, is a Warnier-Orr diagram which will detail the process of eating a restaurant dinner. Since we have an objective in mind, we should be able to tell when we are finished --i.e. when we have the diagram which explains the process. At this point, we are ready to begin to "take the process apart."

We would start by labeling a very large process bracket "How to eat dinner at a restaurant," or maybe just "Restaurant Dinner."

Then, we can start to break down that process of eating dinner into several smaller, easier to understand processes, because remember, we are writing this for a very simple minded computer who gets very confused if we ask it to do too much at a single time. We want to end up with a simple list of instructions that it will be able to follow.

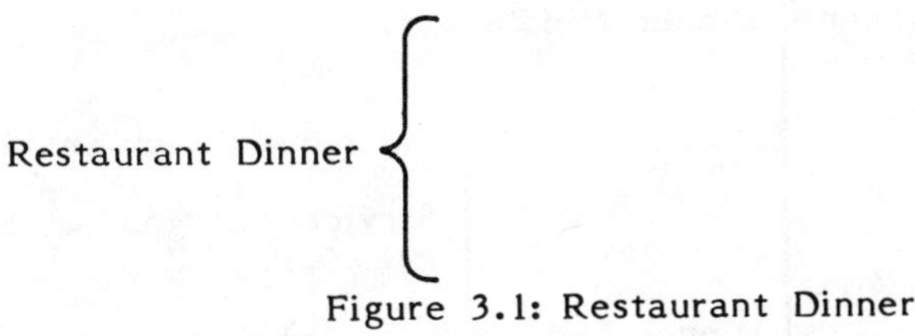


Figure 3.1: Restaurant Dinner

We know from experience that large processes can always be broken up into at least three pieces: the beginning of the process, the middle of the process, and the end of the process. So these are the first pieces that we will break up "Restaurant Dinner" into.

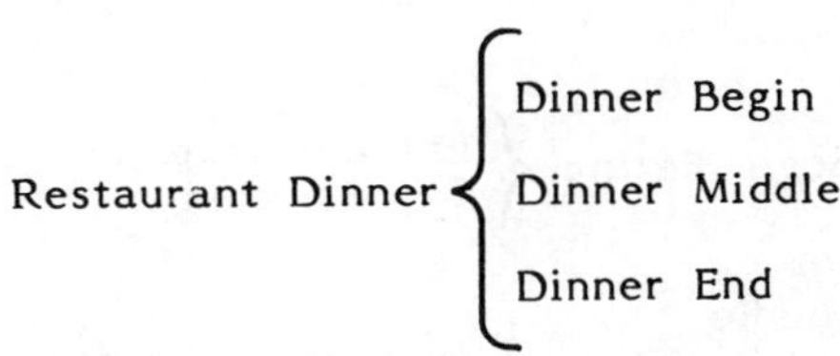


Figure 3.1a

To begin Dinner, you need to look at the menu, decide what you want to eat, order your food, and place your napkin in your lap. At the end of the Dinner, you'll want to put the napkin back onto the table, decide whether or not to leave the waiter or waitress a tip, and then pay for your meal.

Well, this solves a bit of the process, but we still have the middle of the meal to define. We'll call it "Eat Dinner", since that is what we have to do between putting a napkin in our lap and putting it back onto the table. This process of "Eating Dinner" can also be broken down into a beginning, a middle, and an end. These are shown in Figure 3.1c.

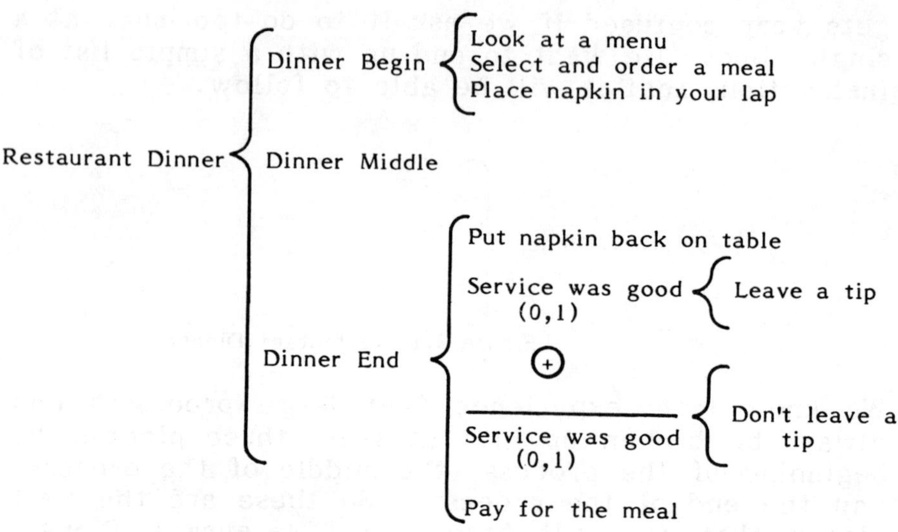


Figure 3.1b

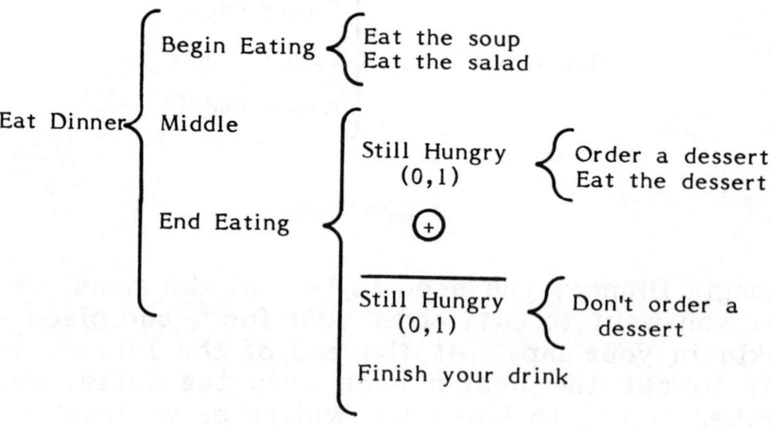


Figure 3.1c

Again, between the time that you eat your salad and the time that you select your dessert, there remains the task of eating the main courses of the meal. For this to be a generalized diagram for eating any dinner, we'll show that there can be a variable "c" number of courses. This is shown in Overlay 3.1d.

Courses (1,c) { Eat this course
Sip your drink

Figure 3.1.d

We are going to assume at this point that out simple-minded computer can understand all of our final instructions on the diagram. Of course, if they did not know, for instance, how to look at a

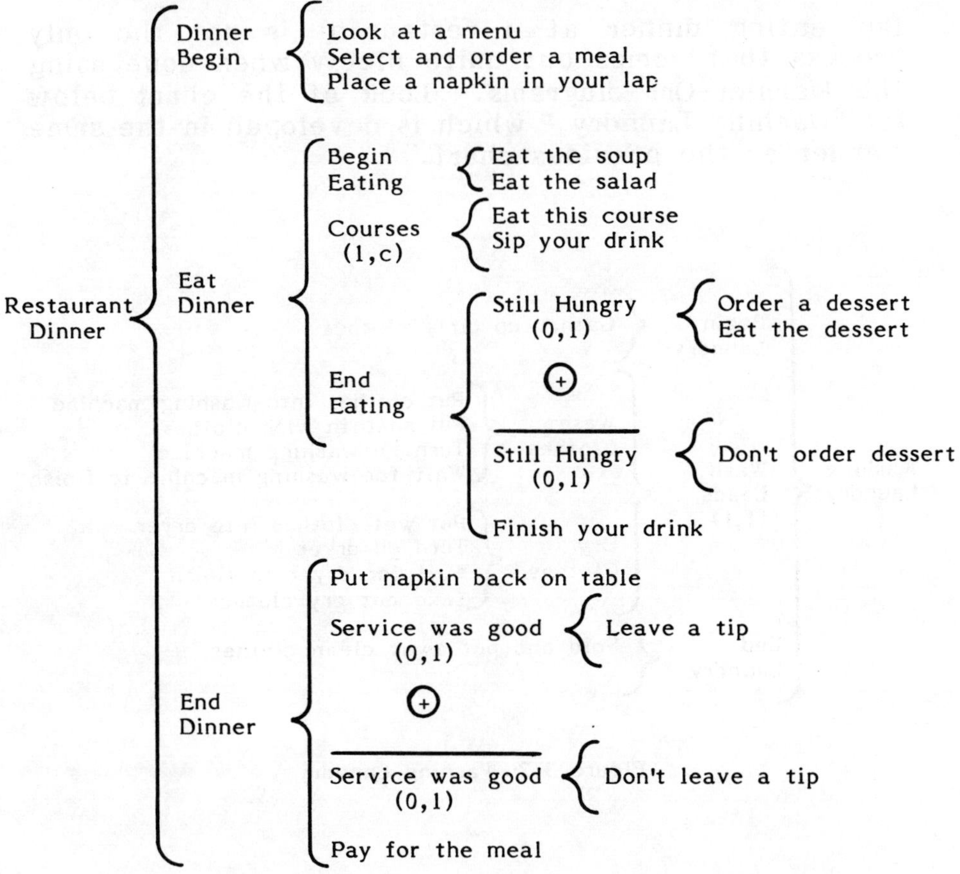


Figure 3.1e: Restaurant Dinner Process

menu and decide what to eat, then we would have to break that process down even further into even simpler instructions. With a computer, it is much easier to tell when you are done. The final instructions have to be statements that the computer will accept and understand.

Since all of this diagram is now broken down into small enough pieces for our computer to understand, we do not need to break it down any further. This represents the completed Warnier-Orr diagram for the process of eating dinner at a restaurant. It charts a time and a place for every function that must occur.

But eating dinner at a restaurant is not the only process that comes out quite nicely when done using the Warnier-Orr diagrams. Look at the chart below for "Washing Laundry," which is developed in the same manner as the previous chart.

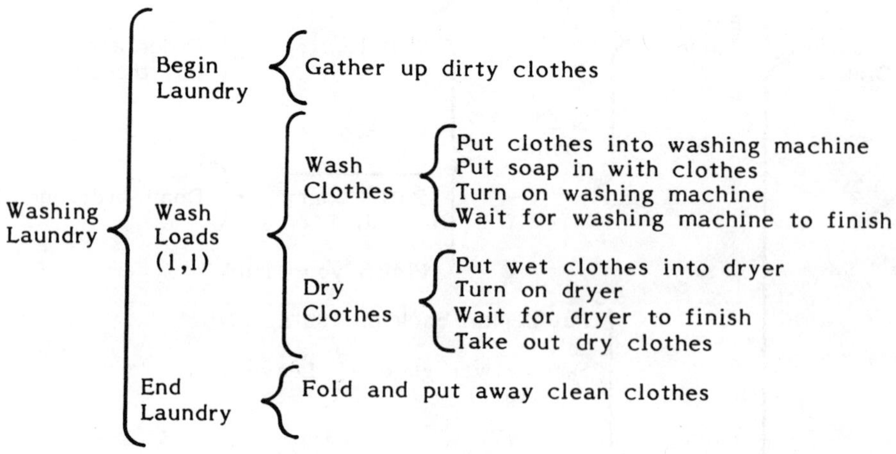


Figure 3.2: Washing Laundry

Or consider the following diagram that shows how to "Bake a Cake."

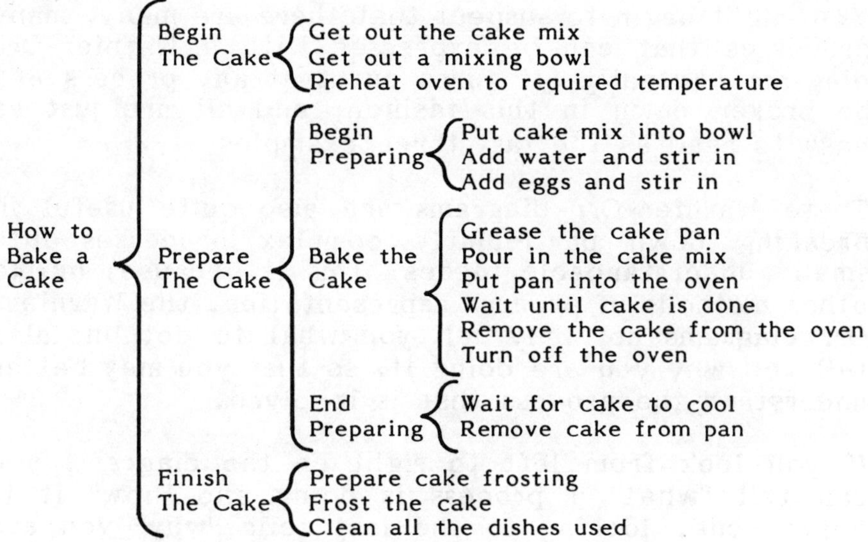


Figure 3.3: How to Bake a Cake

**Or this diagram which shows how to change a flat tire:**

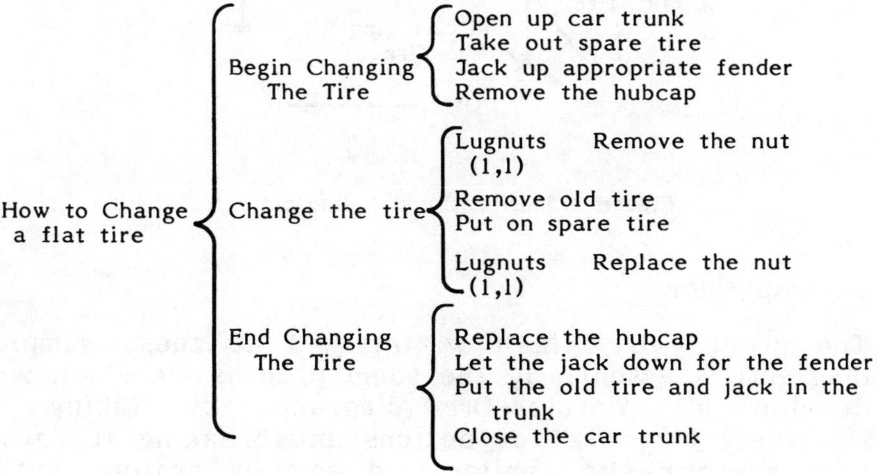


Figure 3.4: How To Change A Tire

You might begin to suspect that there are many, many processes that can be expressed with a Warnier-Orr diagram. Actually, it turns out that any process can be broken down in this fashion, and all are just as easy to read as the last three examples.

These Warnier-Orr diagrams are also quite useful in breaking down particularly complex processes into small, understandable pieces. This is because, unlike other methods of process representation, the Warnier-Orr diagrams not only tell you what to do, but also tell you why you are doing it, so that you may better understand the process that is involved.

If you look from left to right on the diagram, you can tell "what" a process is doing and "how" it is being done, looking to the left tells "why" you are doing it, and looking down from the top to the bottom will tell you the order in which to do it, or the "when."

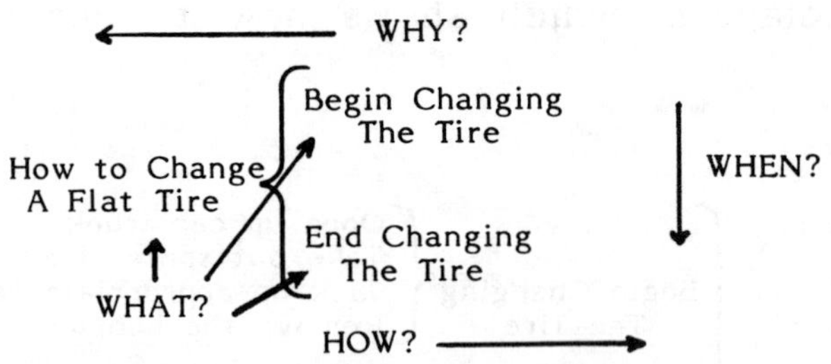


Figure 3.5: Directional Indicators

## Decomposition

The process by which we arrived at these sample diagrams is essentially the same process by which we develop all Warnier-Orr diagrams: by taking a relatively large set of actions and breaking it down into successively smaller and smaller actions until finally we are left with only simple, elemental instructions that a computer can understand.

This method of breaking large actions into small actions is known more formally as the process of decomposition. It is also sometimes called top-down design, because it starts at the 'top,' the highest level of conceptualization, and then proceeds to work its way 'down' deeper and deeper into the problem. Top-down design has been around in the computer industry for quite a few years in one form or another, and data processing people will tell you that top-down design is the best way to design. It is not. It is the only way to design.

But where is it that we come to know just how a particular process breaks down or decomposes? How do we know just what pieces that it breaks down into. With the Warnier-Orr techniques, this is not just a matter of intuition; there are certain rules and criteria for breaking apart a process in a very refined and orderly way. We'll start to look at those rules in the following chapter.

## EXERCISES

1. Define the terms sequence, alternation, repetition, top-down, and decomposition.

2. Using the examples in the chapter as a guide, draw a simple Warnier-Orr diagram of a common household or business action. For example, reading the newspaper, fixing dinner, getting up in the morning, mixing a favorite drink, etc.

3. In all of the repetitive structures that we have seen so far, they have each been conditioned by the notation "(1,n)." Do you see any difference between that notation and one of "(0,n)?" Is there any reason that you can think of that we might need the different notation?

# 4

# The Methodology: Data Structures

## Logical Design Methodology

When the computer industry first began, no one suspected that there might be a need to have a step-by-step process allowing just anyone to become a computer programmer. After all, the early computing machines were very complicated, they weren't very reliable with respect to the hardware, there weren't very many of them around, and they were difficult to program--difficult because they were of such a construction that their programmers had to have a great deal of knowledge about the physical characteristics of the computer in order to program it correctly. Programmers had to be careful to not only write programs that got the right answers, but they had to be careful that they didn't issue any commands that could cause the computer to physically damage itself.

But as the years went by and the computers became more reliable, more numerous and more accessible, it became obvious that a great number of people would, at one time or another in their lives, have to write some sort of a program for some sort of a computer.

In order to be able to do this, there had to be a method developed which would

1. Be easy to learn
2. Be easy to use
3. Produce correct processes
4. Produce consistent results
5. Allow easy maintenance

Necessity is indeed the mother of invention, and out of this great need emerged the methodology that we are about to explore. This is a "cookbook" methodology, that has well defined steps and procedures for developing processes that can be turned into correct programs. We begin the examination of the methodology with this chapter.

## Hierarchy

Before we get into the process of defining formally the methods for process design, there is very important concept that needs to be explored in a bit of detail. That concept is known as hierarchy.

The dictionary defines a hierarchy as "a graded rank or series," but that definition, aside from being useless as far as we are concerned, is not quite what we need in the process design field. As was said in an earlier chapter, hierarchy can basically be defined as the relationship between a set and one of its subsets. This is really the definition that we need to understand.

Perhaps the best way to get a feel for the concept of hierarchy is to see an example of it as it pertains to our particular interest. To start with, let's take a non-data processing example. Let's look at the game of football.

Now if someone were to tell you that football is a hierarchically organized and very well structured game, you might take issue with that. After all, if you watch a typical game, football appears to be decidedly unstructured--just two random but opposing masses of humanity trying to kill each other over an inflated oblong ball.

But surprisingly enough, the game of football is quite structured in a hierarchical fashion. You see, each football season is made up of a number of games. Each game is made up of two halves, called, oddly enough, the "first half" and the "second half." Each of those halves, in turn, is divided up into two quarters. This is a hierarchy, and we represent it on a Warnier-Orr diagram like this:

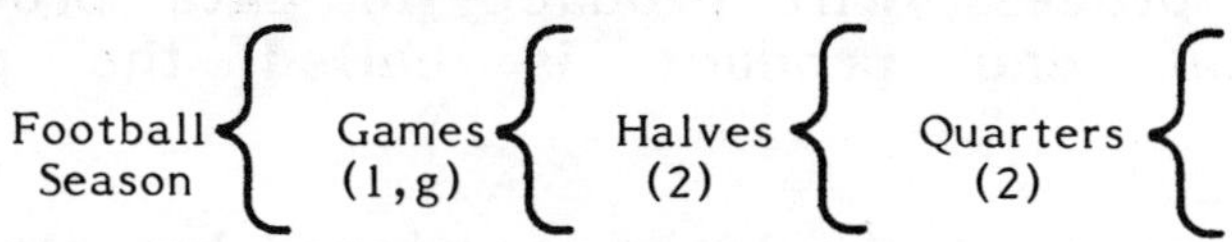


Figure 4.1: Football Hierarchy

So really, what we mean by hierarchy is not anything complicated or even new. It is a concept that you've probably been familiar with for a long time, even though you probably didn't call it by that name.

## Getting Started

In the last chapter we looked at some simple, everyday processes as they would be expressed in Warnier-Orr diagram form. The technique for decomposing those diagrams into their proper segments was really only hinted at, though. In fact, it might even appear from the work in the last chapter that breaking processes down is a matter of skill and intuition.

But the techniques for decomposition are not as random and intuitive as they might seem. There are quite a few well defined and precise rules that we can use to develop the Warnier-Orr diagram for any given process. The first goal for our design process is to develop and examine what is called the "data structure" of our problem. But in order to do that, we must first

**STEP 1:** Define the Process' "Outputs".

This is the first step in the design process. And, since all of the rest of our work is dependent upon how well we do this step, it is also the most important.

In order to develop the data structure of a process, which we said was what we really want at this point, we need to do a careful analysis of the final product that our process will produce--in data processing terms that end product is called the process "output."

As a side note, it should be mentioned here that this entire Warnier-Orr methodology is often called "output oriented analysis," because of the fact that it begins works backwards from the final product to the basic building blocks. The techniques' very name implies the importance of starting with the output, and this is a principle that cannot be stressed enough. After all, you cannot get somewhere if you do not know where you are going; you cannot build something if you do not know what it should look like when you are done.

## Using Data Structures

The data structure of a computer application is completely and absolutely dependent upon the output of that particular application.

The output of an application, or in this case, a computer program, can be many things. That output could be, for example, a monthly financial statement; it could be a projected yearly budget; it could be a game of checkers; or it could be a piece of music. In short, the output of a program can be just about anything that you can imagine, and is limited only by the physical characteristics of the computer that you happen to be using; it is not limited by the logic of the problem. What is meant by that statement is that obviously, you cannot make a computer jump across the room if it doesn't have any legs, or play a piece of music if it does not have some facility to produce a sound. But if you do have the proper equipment, you should be able to program that equipment to do anything it is capable of doing. (There is a class of problems which are provably unsolvable, but they are typically of such an esoteric nature that the average computer program designer need not worry about them.)

Since each program has a different output, they obviously each have a different data structure, and finding that data structure is usually quite easy.

```
                          SAVINGS ACCOUNT ACTIVITY
                  FOR THE YEAR ENDING DECEMBER 31, 1977

ACCOUNT # 15-555-97

 JANUARY ACTIVITY                               BALANCE FORWARD OF $212.10

        DATE   ACTION                  DR         CR           BALANCE
          1    DEPOSIT              100.00                      312.10
          3    WITHDRAWAL                        23.13          288.97
          7    WITHDRAWAL                        10.00          278.97
         12    DEPOSIT              270.00                      548.97
               .                                                  .
               .                                                  .
               .                                                  .
         30    DEPOSIT              400.00                      650.11
                                 ---------  ---------       ----------
 FOR THE MONTH OF JANUARY         1,234.56     796.55           650.11

 FEBRUARY ACTIVITY                              BALANCE FORWARD OF $650.11
               .                      .          .                .
               .

                                 ---------  ---------       ----------
 TOTAL FOR ACCOUNT # 15-555-97   12,234.87  11,456.34           990.63


ACCOUNT # 15-666-98
               .                      .          .                .
               .
                                 ---------  ---------       ---------
 TOTAL FOR ACCOUNT # 15-666-98   11,768.67  11,976.54           244.13

                                 ---------  ---------       ----------
 TOTALS FOR 1977                 24,003.54  23,432.88         1,234.76
```

Figure 4.2 - Savings Account Activity Report

Examine Figure 4.2 as an example of a report that we might want our computer to print.

This report would show for each year, all of accounts that we had. For each account, the report would show each months' activity and the year end balance for that account. For each month, the report would show the beginning and the ending monthly balance, and it would show the daily activity and the current balance for the account.

If you wanted to be able to produce this report without a computer (with just a pen and paper and an adding machine, say), you would want to have all of the deposits and withdrawals for that year written on individual slips of paper and sorted into separate piles for each account. Within each of those piles you would want the transactions sorted by month and by day.

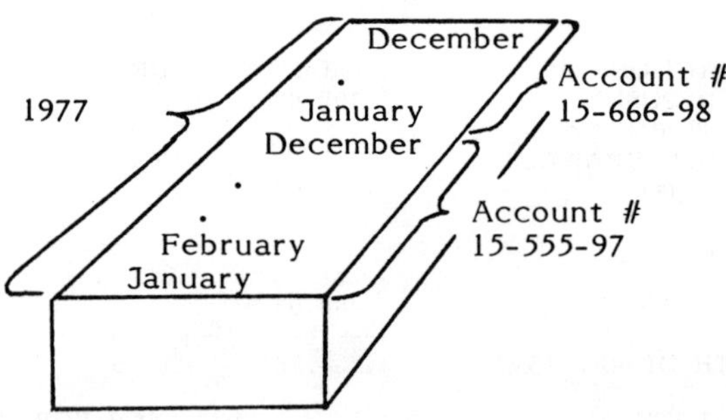


Figure 4.3:Sorted Report Records

If you had the information in this order, then producing the report would be fairly easy, right? You would have all of the information that you need for the report in the order in which you would use it. Adding the totals up and writing them down would be almost a trivial exercise. For each transaction you would add the amount to a monthly subtotal, which is then added at the end of the month to an account subtotal, all of which are added to produce the grand total.

This report, like the game of football that we discussed earlier, is said to be organized "hierarchically," because it is broken into a series of levels or cycles, each of which is contained within all of the levels 'above' it. This logical hierarchy is represented on a Warnier-Orr diagram this way.

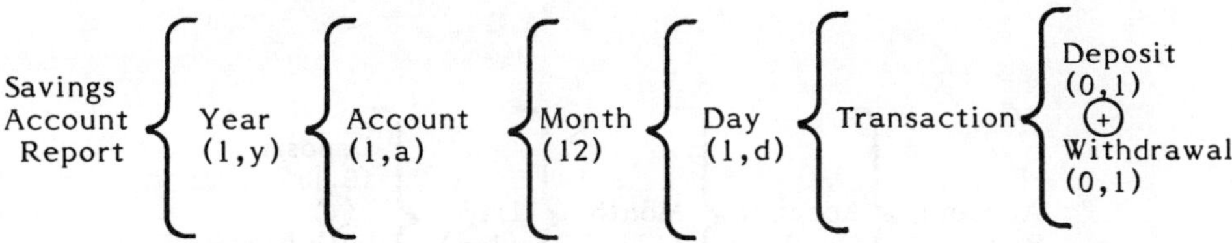


Figure 4.4:Account Report Hierarchy

The diagram indicates that this report is organized by years; within years by accounts; within accounts by months; within months by days; and within days by transactions. The "number of times" that each level of the hierarchy occurs is also shown. Note that although "Transaction" occurs once per day, no "number of times" indication appears. We assume that if no "number of times" notation is apparent then the entry occurs just one time.

Finding the data structure of the report is a process that reaches back to some of the original concepts that Warnier put forth in his "Laws for the Construction of Programs," work--called L.C.P. for short. Warnier tells us that we should

1. Look for repetition
2. Look for alternation

And, from the work done by Ken Orr and his group we have the following rule:

3.) Look for logical groups

If we look at Figure 4.1, we can see immediately that for our account report, within each year the "Account" process is repeated. So are the "Month" and "Day" processes. Within "Day," however, the "Transactions" are not repeated, but consist of either a "Deposit" or a "Withdrawal" but not both on any single day. This is an alternative structure. So, if we were to draw the data structure for this report using only Warnier's rules for L.C.P., we would get the following diagram:

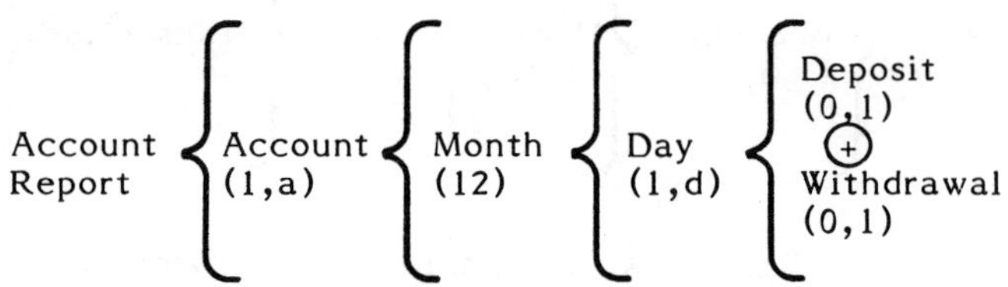


Figure 4.5: L.C.P. Data Structure

If we add the third rule, it becomes apparent that the report is grouped first by the logical group "Year", and that the "Deposits" and the "Withdrawals" together make up the logical group "Transactions," so we add these to our data structure.

What we obtain is, of course, the diagram that is shown in Figure 4.3. This is a more complete data structure and it is the one that we would rather have as we continue on into the next phase of analysis. It should be stressed that logically, both of these diagrams depict the correct data structure; the fuller diagram just shows a few more useful details.

It constitutes the logical "skeleton" that we will build all of the rest our analysis around. But before we do that, however, let's look at a few more data structures.

The easiest data structures to spot are ususally to be found in reports like the one above, so we'll look at those first. A very simple report with an easy to see data structure would be:

```
             ACME WIDGET COMPANY
              FEBRUARY 28, 1978

  PLANT #1                          UNITS PRODUCED
       FEB. 1                             27
       FEB. 2                             12
       FEB. 3                             15
       FEB. 6                             17
       FEB. 7                             11
         .                                 .
         .                                 .
         .                                 .
       FEB. 28                            22
                                        ------
  TOTAL FOR PLANT #1                     213

  PLANT #2
         .                                 .
         .                                 .
         .                                 .
                                        ------
GRAND TOTAL                              411
```

Figure 4.6: Acme Widget Company

If we examine this report, we can see quite readily that it also is organized hierarchically; by Month, by Plant, and by Day. This hierarchy is expressed on a Warnier-Orr diagram in the same way as the previous report.

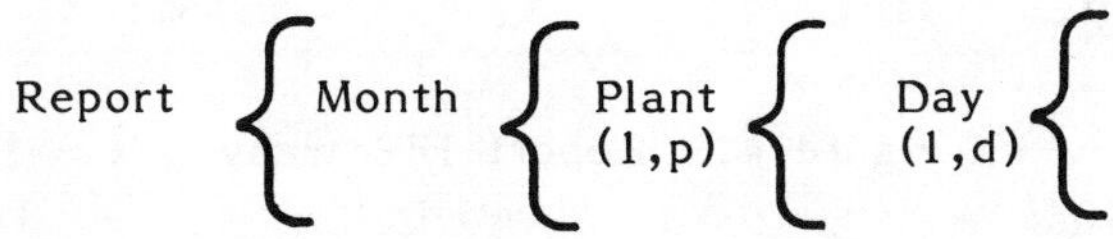

```
Report { Month { Plant { Day {
                 (1,p)   (1,d)
```

Figure 4.7: Report Hierarchy

Another report that we might want to print looks like this:

```
            AJAX PUMP COMPANY
          FOR FISCAL YEAR 1977

    JULY                              SALES    PROFIT
       DIVISION I
           SECTION A                 213.11     76.90
           SECTION B                 378.33    127.21
              .                         .         .
              .                         .         .
       TOTAL FOR DIVISION I        1,265.66    452.93

       DIVISION II
              .                         .         .
              .                         .         .

    TOTAL FOR JULY                 3,811.93  1,409.30

    AUGUST                            SALES    PROFIT
              .                         .         .
              .                         .         .

GRAND TOTAL                       36,217.98  9,182.17
```

Figure 4.8: AJAX PUMP COMPANY

Again, this report is organized hierarchically: by year, by month, by division, and by section. The data structure should look the same.

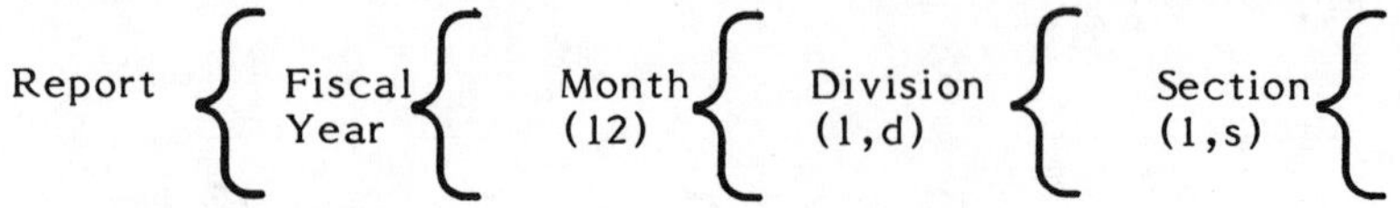

```
Report { Fiscal { Month { Division { Section {
         Year     (12)    (1,d)      (1,s)
```

Figure 4.9: Report Hierarchy

But eventually, we'll want to be able to find the data structure of a task other than a simple report. After all, reports are only a tiny fraction of the possible jobs you can do with a computer. Let's see what the data structure is for another important microcomputer application: a game. If you look back at Exercise 3 for Chapter 2, you'll find the rules for a simple game, the game of "BUG." Briefly, the game is played by two or more players, who take turns rolling a die. Each number of the die corresponds to a piece of the BUG's body, and the first player to complete a BUG wins the game. The conditions for receiving a BUG part are detailed in the Exercise.

For a game like BUG to be implemented on a computer, we would probably have the computer roll the die and then report any BUG part that the player receives. At the end of each game, the computer would report the winner. So the rolling of the die, the report of the BUG parts, and the reporting of the winner are the outputs of a BUG program.

As you might suspect, the game of BUG also has a data structure, which looks a lot like the hierarchical structures we have seen before.

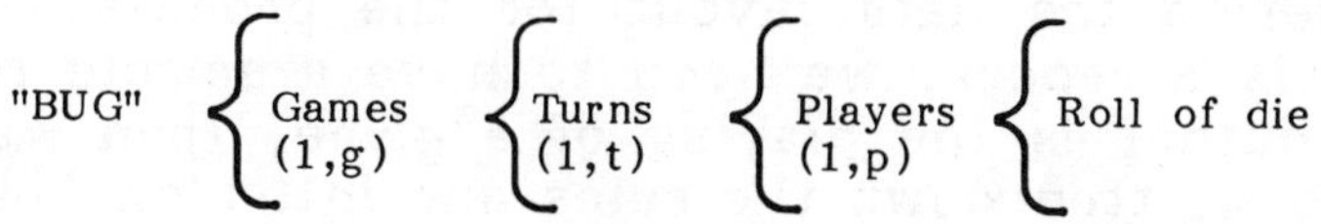

"BUG" { Games (1,g) { Turns (1,t) { Players (1,p) { Roll of die

Figure 4.10: BUG Game Hierarchy

Each time that someone plays "BUG," it is divided up into one or more games; each game is made up of one or more turns by one or more players. So that this game, although very different in function and form from the reports we looked at earlier, still has a distinct and definable data structure. Actually, the "number of times" notation for "Turns" is "(12,t)," since according to the rules it will take at least twelve turns before anyone can possibly win the game, but "(1,t)" is standard notation and we'll use it instead to avoid confusion over terminology.

So, to formalize the techniques that we've been talking about in this chapter, let's list the steps required for the process of defining the outputs of a process.

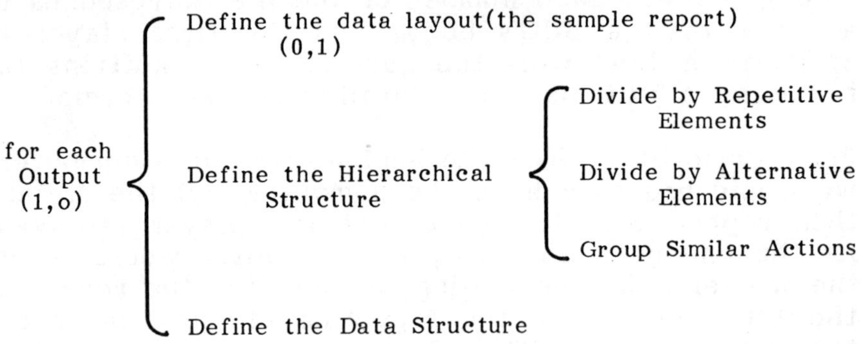


Figure 4.11: Definition of Outputs

This diagram tells us that for each output, we must first define the data layout for the process. If the output is a report, we need to have a sample report. If the output is the playing of a game, then we need to have written down the rules and intended functions of the game. Sometimes, however, the sample report does not need to be developed. In the business world, often times such samples are made up already by the time that the designer gets the problem. That is the reason for the "(0,1)" notation beneath this step on the diagram.

Then, after having defined a data layout for the output, the diagram tells us that we need to define that output's hierarchical structure. We find the hierarchical structure by looking for repetitive structures, alternative structures, and logical groupings.

So you see that finding the data structure for any particular process is not at all difficult. It does, however, require quite a bit of practice. Therefore, working the exercises for this chapter is very strongly recommended.

## EXERCISES

For each of the following reports, draw the Warnier-Orr diagram of it's data structure.

1.)

```
                    REPORT #1

DEPARTMENT 1                  COST
    PROJECT A               286.98
    PROJECT B               125.53
        .                      .
        .                      .
DEPARTMENT 1 TOTAL         1597.48

DEPARTMENT 2
        .                      .
        .                      .
DEPARTMENT 2 TOTAL         1648.26

GRAND TOTAL                3245.74
```

2.)

```
                    REPORT #2

JANUARY                                 SALES
   DIVISION 1
      SECTION A
         EMPLOYEE 10
            JAN 1                       13.25
            JAN 2                       12.24
              .                           .
              .                           .
         TOTAL FOR EMPLOYEE 10          89.25

         EMPLOYEE 15
              .                           .
              .                           .
      TOTAL FOR SECTION A            1,236.86

      SECTION B
              .                           .
   TOTAL FOR DIVISION 1              9,754.46

   DIVISION 2
              .                           .
TOTAL FOR JANUARY                  164,567.45
```

3.) Draw the Warnier-Orr diagrams for the data structure of the following games:

a. Checkers
b. Baseball
c. Blackjack (or "21")

# 5

# The Methodology: Logical Data Bases Part One

## LOGICAL OUTPUT STRUCTURES

### Getting It Right

Almost everyone has heard the old story of the slow-witted cowboy who one day tells his friends, "I really feel good today. I think I'll go into town, kick a few cattle rustlers around and kiss me a mess of pretty girls," and then turns and rides off in a cloud of dust. One friend turns to the other and says "Boy, I sure hope he gets it right this time!"

Our friend the cowboy seems to have a bit of a problem "getting it right," and consequently he has his troubles. "Getting it right" can be a problem in process design also. Having the data structure for a job that you want to do is a very good start, but you will still need to add a little bit more information to the structure before you can do much of anything useful with it. That information, coupled with a touch of good old-fashioned logic will get the job done and will "get it right." You will not only have a design that works, but you will have a logically correct design that can be converted into a working computer program; one that you can be absolutely sure of.

## Logical Data Base

Once you have defined the data structure for a particular job using the techniques presented in the last chapter, the next step requires that we

**STEP 2:** Define the Logical Data Base

This is the next step in our process development methodology. The Logical Data Base, or LDB as it will be called occasionally, is the end product of this next series of developmental steps. We shall take the so-called "skeleton" of our problem and begin to flesh it out a bit.

The Logical Data Base is defined to be "all of the data needed to correctly produce the output(s) desired." We develop the Logical Data Base for an output in a predefined and predictable manner. We begin with that outputs' data structure as it was developed, and copy or map onto it all of the 'data elements' that appear on the output. For the savings account report that appears in Figure 4.2, the 'data elements' are things like the yearly credit total, the credit amount, the monthly debit total, the yearly current balance, all of the titles and headings, etc.

The first step that we must take is to make a list of all of the data elements that appear on the report. That list, again for the savings account report of Figure 4.1, is shown in Figure 5.1.

Two conventions that we use for the data elements list are:

1. Data fields (actual numbers and such) in small letters
2. Titles and headings in capitals and enclosed in quotes

After we get the list of data elements, we are ready to map those elements onto the data structure that we've already developed. Our mapping routine is basically a simple question: "Where does this element occur in the data structure?"

"SAVINGS ACCOUNT ACTIVITY"
"FOR THE YEAR ENDED"
year end date
"ACCOUNT #"
account number
month name
"ACTIVITY"
"BALANCE FORWARD OF"
balance forward amount
"DATE"
"ACTION"
"DR"
"CR"
"BALANCE"
date
"DEPOSIT"
"WITHDRAWAL"
deposit amount
withdrawal amount
daily current balance
"FOR THE MONTH OF"
monthly deposit amount
monthly withdrawal amount
monthly current balance
"TOTAL FOR ACCOUNT"
account deposit amount
account withdrawal amount
account current balance
"TOTALS FOR"
year number
yearly deposit amount
yearly withdrawal amount
yearly current balance

Figure 5.1: Savings Account Report Data Elements

For instance, the monthly deposit amount occurs at the end of each month. So does the monthly withdrawal amount and the monthly current balance. So we write these data elements onto the data structure at that point, as reflected in Figure 5.2.

Similarly, the yearly deposit amount, the yearly withdrawal amount and the yearly current balance occur at the end of the year. We also include these elements on the structure, as shown in Figure 5.3.

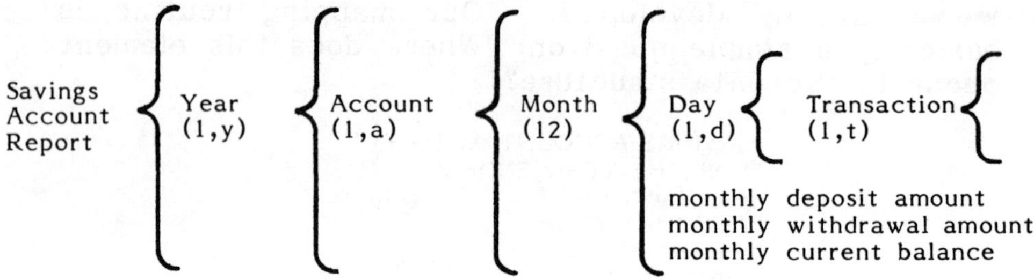


Figure 5.2: Month End Data Elements

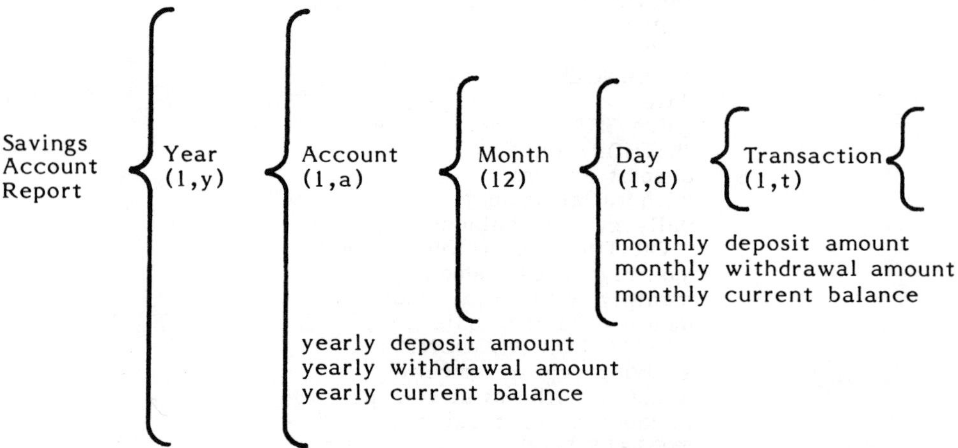


Figure 5.3: Year End Data Elements

When all of the reports' data elements are mapped onto the data structure, we have a completed Warnier-Orr diagram that appears in Figure 5.4.

The diagram of Figure 5.4, with all of the data elements for the report fleshed in, could be called the Logical Data Base for this particular report, since it shows all of the data items needed to produce the report and hence satisfies our definition. However, most of the classical definitions of a Logical Data Base do not accept some of the elements that we have included here. We'll see why in the next chapter. So for now, for lack of a better term, let's call the type of diagram shown in Figure 5.4 the Logical Output Structure or LOS for our process. The Logical Output Structure charts the relationship of all of the data elements of the report with it's logical data structure.

The development of this Logical Output Structure is an important step in our analysis. It allows us to see where in the data structure each of the data elements of our output will occur. Later on, we'll use this information to create the Logical Data Base for the output. We'll also use this diagram to help us write our process structure and to insure that what we've written is correct.

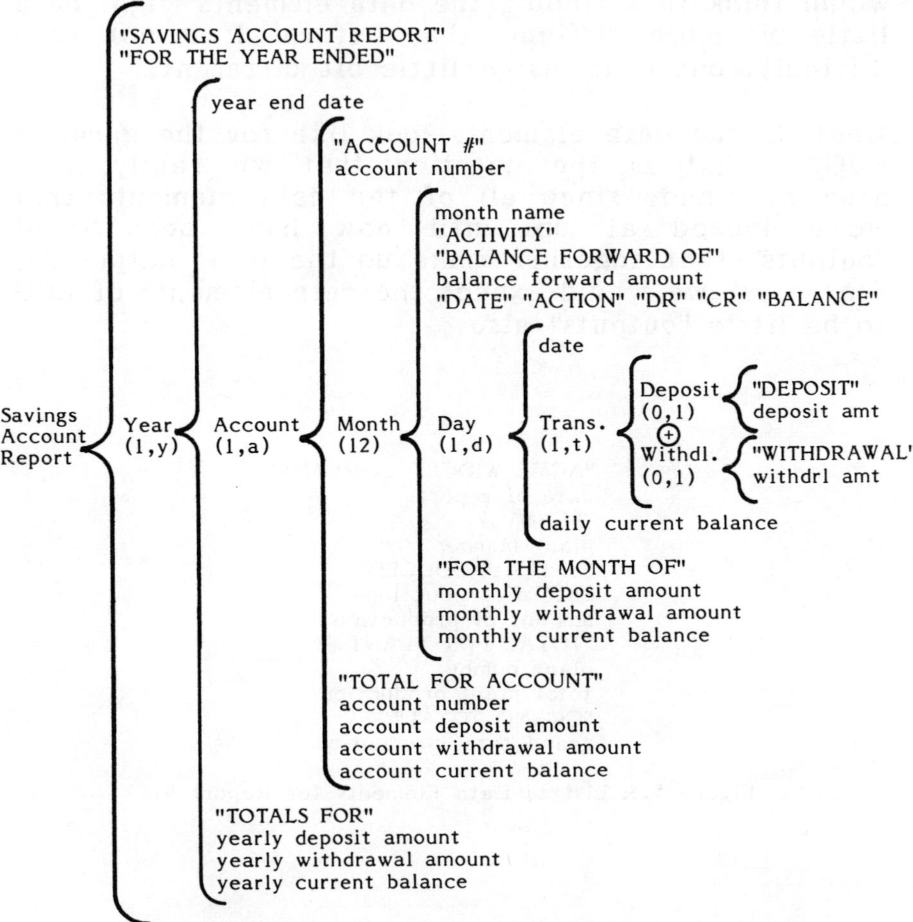


Figure 5.4: Data Structure & Data Elements

If we look at the report of Figure 4.6, we find that its Logical Output Structure is developed in exactly the same manner as before. Again, our final product is called the Logical Output Structure for this report.

For the report in Figure 4.8, the process is exactly the same. These diagrams appear completed in Figures 5.7 and 5.8.

Finally, let's look at the Logical Output Structure for the BUG game that we examined earlier. Since this process is not a fixed, printed report, you would think that finding the data elements might be a little bit more difficult than before. It is not more difficult, but it is just a little bit different.

What do the data elements look like for the game of BUG? That is the question that we really need answer. And, since all of the data elements that we've looked at up until now have been small "outputs" that together make up the total output for a process, we would expect the data elements of BUG to be little "outputs" also.

"ACME WIDGET COMPANY"
date of report
"PLANT #"
plant number
"UNITS PRODUCED"
date of production
amount of production
"TOTAL FOR PLANT #"
plant number
total plant production
"GRAND TOTAL"
grand total production

Figure 5.5: List of Data Elements for Report 4.6

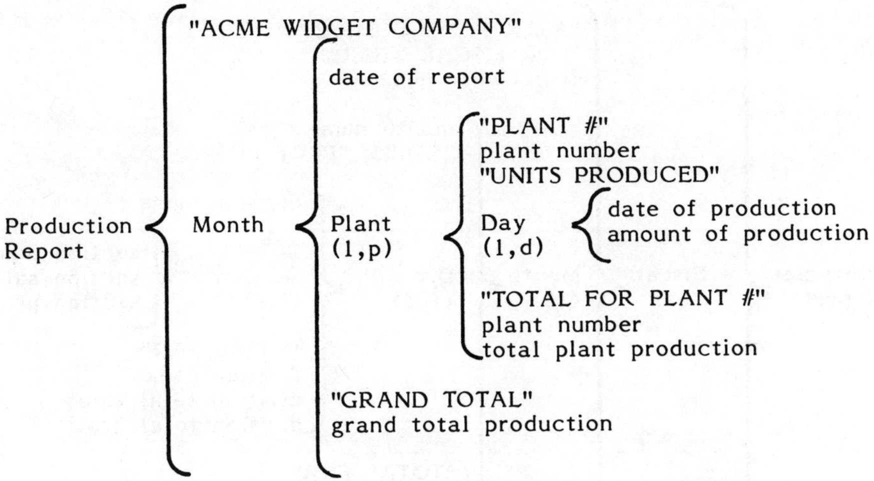


Figure 5.6: Logical Output Structure for Report 4.6

"ACME PUMP COMPANY"
"FOR FISCAL YEAR"
fiscal year number
month name
"SALES"
"PROFIT"
division name
section name
section sales
section profit
"TOTAL FOR"
division name
division total sales
division total profit
"TOTAL FOR"
month name
monthly total sales
monthly total profit
"GRAND TOTAL"
grand total sales
grand total profit

Figure 5.7: List of Data Elements for Report 4.8

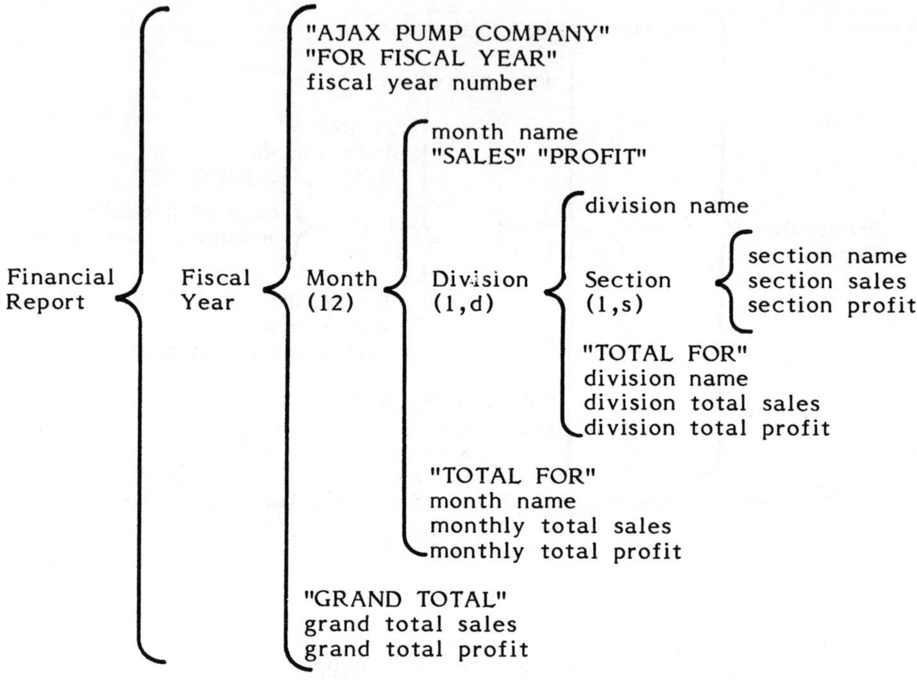


Figure 5.8: Logical Output Structure for Report 4.8

If you think about it, there are really only two small outputs essential to this game, which in turn complete the overall output: the roll of the die for each player and the awarding of the corresponding piece of the BUG that the roll represents. Of course, if we are playing this game with a computer, we'll want it to "roll the die" (i.e., pick a random number between one and six) for us and tell us what part of the BUG we get. These are the only really necessary outputs to the game of BUG, however, there are traditionally two more outputs that we should include. At the beginning of the game we will want the computer to explain the rules and at the end of the game declare the winner and print out a "CONGRATULATIONS" message to the winner. These elements, although not essential to the playing of our game, are usually found in all computer games. We'll list these data elements with the two vital data elements discussed before.

roll of the die
part of bug body
"EXPLANATION OF RULES..."
"CONGRATULATIONS..."

Figure 5.9: BUG Game Data Elements

So that when we map the data elements for the game of BUG onto the data structure for the game, we get

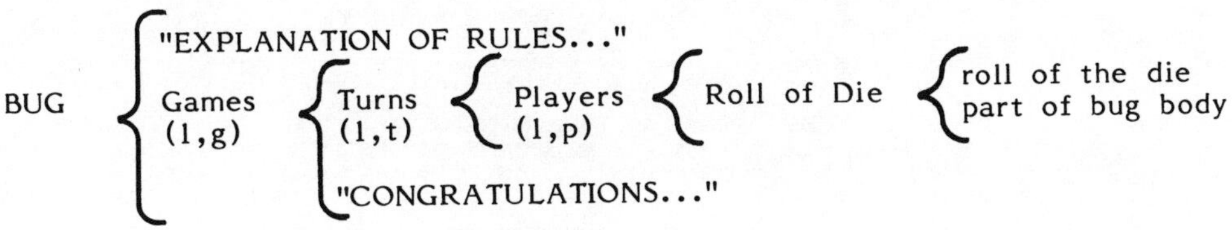

- BUG
  - "EXPLANATION OF RULES..."
  - Games (1,g)
    - Turns (1,t)
      - Players (1,p)
        - Roll of Die
          - roll of the die
          - part of bug body
    - "CONGRATULATIONS..."

Figure 5.10: "BUG" Logical Output Structure

This structure is still called the Logical Output Structure for the game of BUG. It lists the time and the place that each important output is produced, and will therefore be essential to the work that will follow.

In the next chapter, we'll see how to convert a Logical Output Structure like those that we have derived here to a Logical Data Base for a process.

## EXERCISES

1. For both Exercises 4.1 and 4.2, complete the list of data elements and the Logical Output Structure for that report.

# 6

# The Methodology: Logical Data Bases Part Two

## DATA BASE DESIGN

### Logical Output Structure vs. Logical Data Base

By now, the reader should be able to take a process for which some output is desired, and develop a Logical Output Structure for it. This ability is crucial to the success of the rest of the design methodology. However, ultimately what the second phase of our analysis calls for is not just a Logical Output Structure, but instead a Logical Data Base, which is a little bit different.

In order to get the Logical Data Base for a process, it is first necessary to develop the Logical Output Structure for it, as we have done in the last chapter. We said at that time, that for the application in question, the Logical Output Structure could conceivably be called a Logical Data Base, since it showed all of the data elements needed to correctly produce the output.

The reason that we do not just go ahead and call those Logical Output Structures the Logical Data Base for that output is twofold.

First of all, the classical concept of a data base does not include some of the data elements that we show on a LOS. These elements should really be eliminated from the LOS before we do any further development, not only for the sake of consistency with past ideas, but for the added simplicity that it will gain.

The second reason for making a distinction between the LOS and the LDB is probably more important. There are many cases in which further analysis must be done for a process to insure that things aren't left out. This is sometimes the hardest part of the process development methodology. For when things aren't going easily and data elements aren't flowing onto the page like they should, the problem could be that you have neglected to take into account a hidden or invisible hierarchy. We'll discuss this in more detail later in this chapter.

## Beginning the Data Base

The first step that we must take in order to convert a Logical Output Structure into a Logical Data Base requires that we make a distinction between some of the data elements which appear on the structure. We shall find out that some of these elements should be eliminated from the structure in order to develop the Logical Data Base.

## Constant vs. Variable Data Elements

Looking back at the list of data elements in Chapter 5, you will see immediately that there is a distinct difference between two types of the data elements appearing on the Logical Output Structures. One group is capitalized and enclosed within quotes--the other is not capitalized and does not appear in quotes.

The first of those two groups are generally called program constants. All of the report names, the titles, the subheadings, etc. belong to this group. The other group of data elements are usually termed variable data elements. For instance, the data element "yearly deposit amount" is not a name which is printed on the output like a title, but instead the name of a number. And, every time that we want to be able to talk about that number, we'll call it by that name.

We could conceive of that number being held in sort of a slot or a logical "pigeon hole" within the computer--a predefined and fixed place where we could look and always find the number written on a piece of paper.

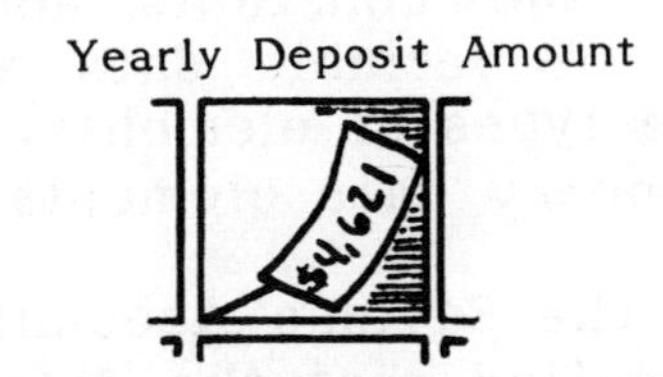


Figure 6.1: Logical Pigeon Hole

In our terminology we'll want to make a very definite distinction between the actual number that we are speaking of and the place in the computer where it is stored. So we'll adopt the convention that "Yearly Deposit Amount," written with only the first letter of each word capitalized, is the "pigeon hole" where we keep the actual number "yearly deposit amount." Actually, in the computer, the number is kept as a series of electronic pulses and not as pencil marks on a piece of paper, but the concept of a fixed location with a number stored in it remains the same.

Since all of the title and heading data elements are called constants, because they do not change in the program, you would logically expect the elements such as "yearly deposit amount" to be called variables, because they can and do change values within the program. The data element "monthly deposit amount" is one number when the month is January; it is another number when the month is February, still another when it is March, etc. But the value of "monthly deposit amount" is always to be found in the pigeon hole "Monthly Deposit Amount." The reason that we make the distinction between the number itself and the place in which the number is kept will become more apparent later on. For now, however, it is sufficient that you realize the difference and be able to recognize which of the two is being referenced.

## Primary vs. Secondary Data Elements

We have already broken the data elements of a problem into two groups: the constants and the variables. Within the group of variable data elements, we can identify two more types of elements. They are called primary and secondary data elements.

Looking again at the Savings Account Activity report in Figure 4.2, we find that the data element "yearly deposit total" is a derived bit of information--it is the result that we obtain by summing up all of the "account deposit totals." The "account deposit total" is also derived; it is the sum of all of the "monthly deposit totals," which in turn is the sum of all of the daily "deposit amounts." But "deposit amount" is not a computed quantity; we cannot find out what the "deposit amount" is if we aren't given it in the first place. Therefore, the element "deposit amount" is called a primary data element. All of the monthly, account and yearly deposit totals are called secondary data elements, since we do not have to be told these figures; we can compute them.

But of what significance is this distinction. Well, if we go back to the Logical Output Structure for this report and remove from it all of the computed data elements, we obtain a Warnier-Orr diagram that appears in Figure 6.2.

This chart is quite interesting. It indicates that if we can obtain just this information exactly when

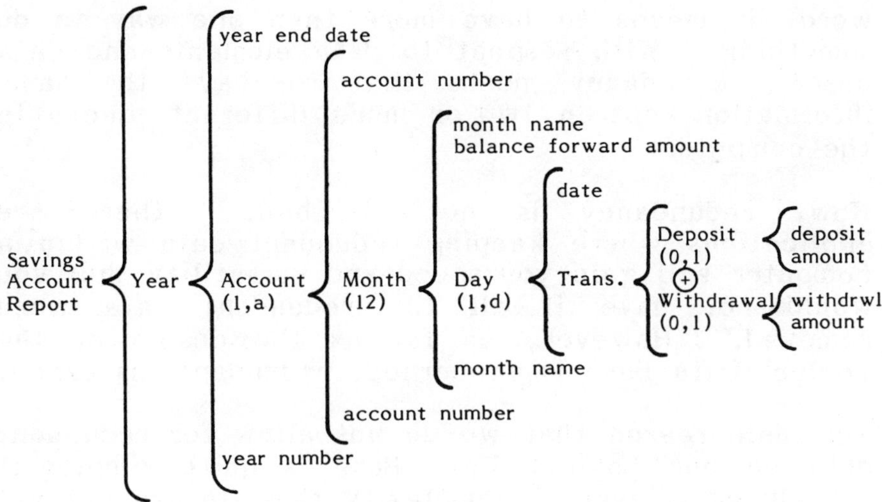


Figure 6.2: Primary Data Elements

it is needed (i.e. if we can find the "month name" and the "balance forward" when we begin the "Month" process; the "deposit amount" when we are doing the "Deposit" process; etc.) then we will have all of the information necessary to correctly produce this report.

This diagram of Figure 6.2 is sometimes called the Logical Input File, or the Logical Input Structure (LIS) since it shows exactly what "inputs" (or primary data elements) that we must capture to produce this report.

Having the Logical Input Structure for the report brings us another step closer to the goal of designing the Logical Data Base. But we're still not there. We need to do two more things to get the LDB.

## Redundancy

Most everyone is familiar with the concept of redundancy. In the way that we normally use the word, it means to have more than one way to do something. With respect to data elements and data bases, redundancy means that we have the same information kept in two or more different places in the computer.

Now, redundancy is not all bad. There are applications where keeping redundant data within a computer will gain you speed and versatility that you would not have if all the redundant data were removed. However, as far as the design of the Logical Data Base is concerned, redundancy is taboo.

The main reason that we do not allow for redundant data on our Logical Data Base is quite simple: it introduces a level of complexity that we are not yet ready to deal with. For if you have the same information stored in more than one place in the computer, then every time that you change that information one place, you must track down all the other places that it occurs and change them also. The failure to systematically change all of the places that information is stored will result in a failure of the system. You will end up with outdated and therefore incorrect data, and producing the correct output will be impossible.

Worrying about redundancy at this point in the design phase is unnecessary. So, we'll eliminate it wherever it occurs. If you look back at the Logical Input Structure, you'll see that there are several data elements which occur redundantly. For instance, "account number" and "month name" both appear twice on the diagram. Also, you might notice that "year number" is contained within the "date," which appears elsewhere and is therefore redundant.

If we eliminate from the Logical Input Structure all but a single occurrence of the redundant items, we will have a more serviceable structure. The single occurrence that we want to leave will always be the first occurrence--for instance, the "month name" will remain at the beginning of the month process, but will be removed from the month end. The reason that we leave the first occurrence of the data item is simple. If we know that we'll need a data item more than once we can save it and use it later.

The Logical Input Structure, with the redundant data elements removed, appears below.

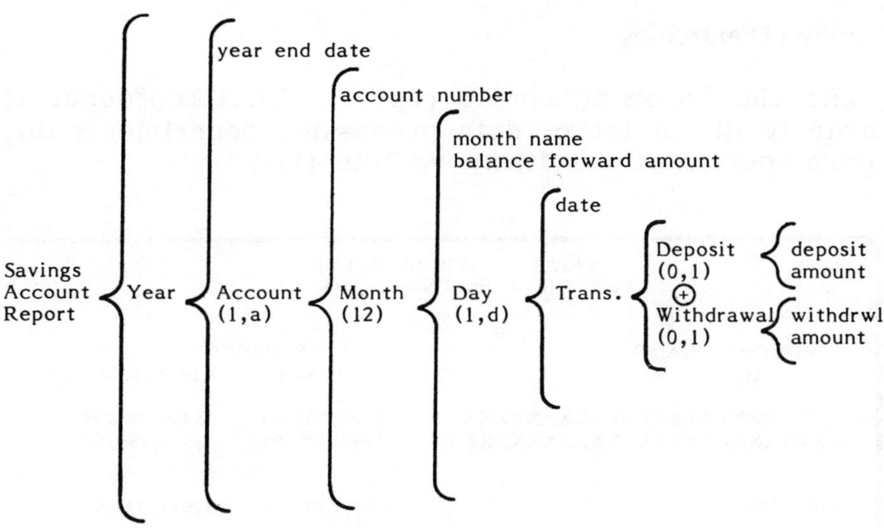


Figure 6.3: LIS Without Redundancies

This chart could very appropriately be called the Logical Data Base for the savings account report given in Figure 4.2. It lists the appropriate hierarchy of the data and it lists the minimal data elements which must be present in order to correctly produce this report.

We produce this Logical Data Base by three steps: we start with the Logical Output Structure for the problem and

1. Develop the Logical Input Structure (eliminate constants)
2. Eliminate secondary (computed) data elements
3. Eliminate redundant data elements

For this particular problem, those were the only required steps. Indeed, for nearly all of the applications that you ever run into, these are the only required steps to produce the Logical Data Base. However, there is a class of problems for which the above three steps will not produce a satisfactory LDB. These are problems which involve something called a hidden hierarchy.

## Hidden Hierarchies

Take the following simple report. We'll reproduce it exactly like a lot of data processing departments do, from specifications drawn up like this:

WEEKLY PAYROLL REPORT
FOR THE WEEK ENDED 77/11/05

| EMPLOYEE NAME | WAGES | |
|---|---|---|
| | WEEKLY | YEAR-TO-DATE |
| XXXXXXXXXXXXXXXXXXXXXXX | $999,999.99 | $999,999.99 |
| XXXXXXXXXXXXXXXXXXXXXXX | $999,999.99 | $999,999.99 |
| GRAND TOTAL | $9,999,999.99 | $9,999,999.99 |

Figure 6.4: Weekly Payroll Report

This kind of a report layout is standard for most data processing shops. It is supposed to show only specific field lengths. That is, it tells us that the EMPLOYEE NAME field is 23 characters wide; the WEEKLY WAGES field for each employee is eight positions wide with two of those positions to the right of the decimal point, with the added information that this field is to be edited so that it prints with a dollar sign and all of its commas and decimal point, etc.

Too often though, this kind of a data layout is interpreted to be the sample output that we discussed in Chapter 4. When this sort of assumption is made, someone begins work on the problem as if the definition of the output was complete. Then, they proceed to produce a Logical Data Base that looks like this:

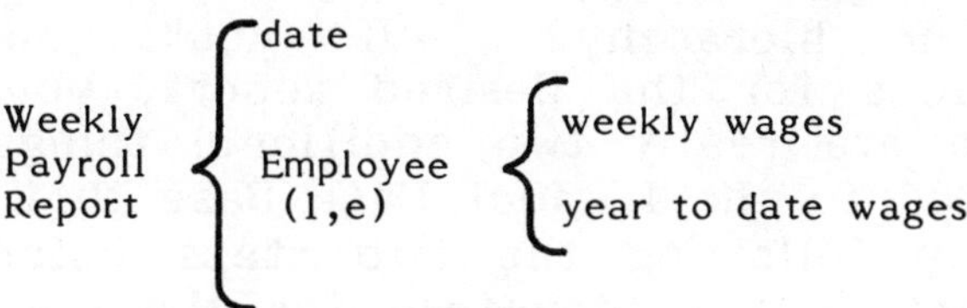


Figure 6.5: Assumed Logical Data Base

The only problem with developing the report from the data layout diagram is that, more often than not, the report is likely to be wrong. The report that we end up producing is this:

WEEKLY PAYROLL REPORT
FOR THE WEEK ENDED 77/11/05

| EMPLOYEE NAME | WAGES | |
|---|---|---|
| | WEEKLY | YEAR-TO-DATE |
| ALLEN, MARY | $150.34 | $7,564.00 |
| ARDEN, FRED | $147.56 | $4,345.78 |
| BISHOP, GARY | $201.99 | $9,549.22 |
| . | . | . |
| . | . | . |
| GRAND TOTAL | $4,311.86 | $39,386.33 |

Figure 6.6: Assumed Final Report

Then, this final report is returned to the person who requested it originally. Only then is it learned that this is not the report that they really wanted. What they really wanted was a report that listed only male employees, and even then, not alphabetically, but from the highest paid weekly amount to the lowest paid weekly amount. Consequently, the data processing people get to do this report over again. This is the kind of trouble that you can get into by using data layout forms as presumed sample outputs.

This also begins to illustrate the problem at hand: the hidden hierarchy. If you'll notice the specifications for the desired report, you will see that there are really two additional things that we need to add to the Logical Data Base that we would not get by following the two steps listed earlier. The Logical Output Structure for the actual report is:

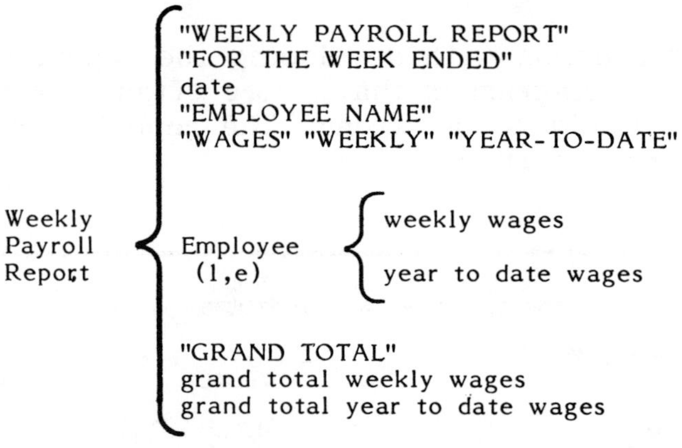


Figure 6.7: Correct Logical Output Structure

So that if we followed only the first three steps, and eliminated the constants, the secondary data elements and the redundant data elements, we would come up with the same Logical Data Base which produced the original wrong report. The actual Logical Data Base should reflect the two hierarchies that are hidden in the Logical Output Structure. They should appear as shown in Figure 6.8.

The one hierarchy, that of the "males only" specification, is reflected as an added level of hierarchy. The other hierarchy, that of listing the largest weekly amount to the smallest weekly amount,

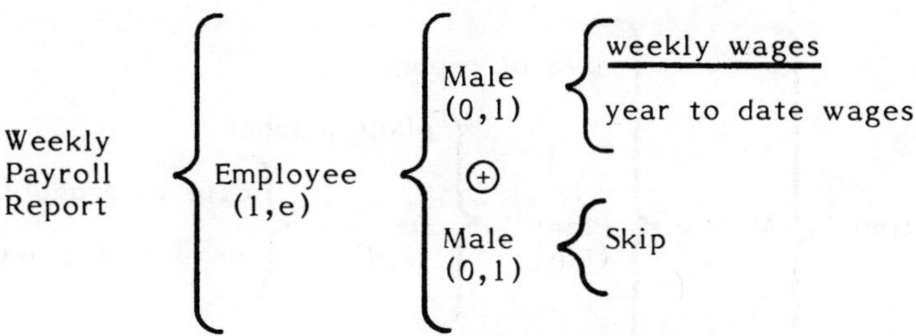


Figure 6.8: Correct Logical Data Base

is indicated by the underlining of the weekly wages data element. The underlining reflects the condition that this is a key field, and that the file from which this report is produced is to be sorted on that field. If no mention is made otherwise, we'll assume that we sort from the highest to the lowest.

The real trick to finding hidden hierarchies boils down to two realizations. If the data elements do not seem to be mapping onto the data structure correctly, that is one clue that you may have missed a hidden hierarchy and that you'll need to go back and rethink the original Logical Output Structure; another is if you realize that after removing the secondary and redundant data elements, the Logical Data Base is insufficiently described to produce the correct output.

## Other Logical Data Bases

Since we have developed the Logical Output Structures for two more reports and one game, let's go ahead and reduce them down to their Logical Data Bases.

The two additional reports develop in the same manner as the first report that we did. From the Logical Output Structure, the constants are removed. Then, the computed elements on the LOS are also removed. Finally, any redundant data elements left on the structure are removed, leaving us with our desired product. The Logical Data Bases for these two reports appear below.

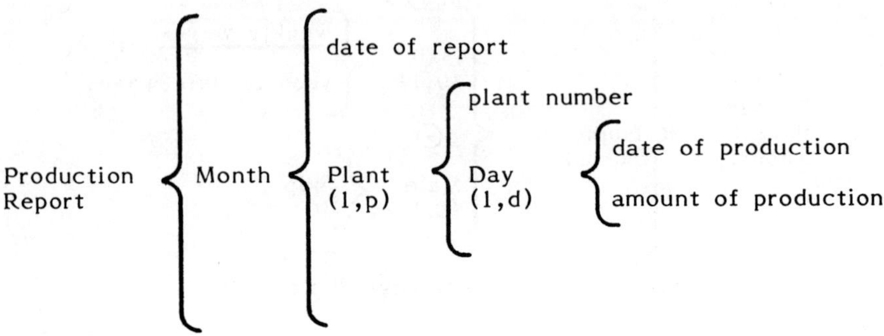


Figure 6.9: LDB for Figure 4.6

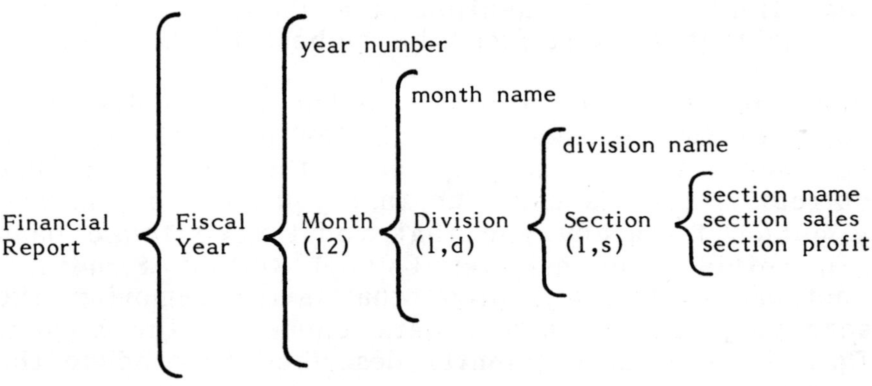


Figure 6.10: LDB for Figure 4.8

This next Logical Data Base is probably going to surprise you. What happens when we eliminate all of the constants, and all of the computed data elements from the LOS of the game of BUG? Well, if you look back at Figure 5.9, you'll see that the only data elements on this output structure are either constants or are computed. Therefore, the Logical Data Base for the game of BUG is nonexistent! Actually, this isn't all that surprising, if you consider that the game could be written to execute all by itself within the computer and report only the winner (actually, the game could play entirely within the computer and not even report the winner). Granted, the game wouldn't be a great deal of fun if it were implemented like that. Consequently, there is usually one data element added to the Logical Output Structure that allow some sort of operator participation in the game. Either we make the roll of the die an element which the operator must determine and then enter, or we simply have the computer report that it is ready to roll the die for the operator and then wait for the operator to push a button before it does. If we want to go with the first option, the LDB looks like:

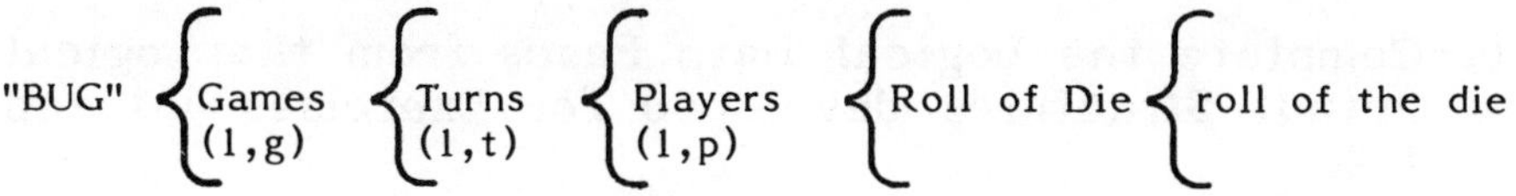

"BUG" { Games (1,g) { Turns (1,t) { Players (1,p) { Roll of Die { roll of the die

Figure 6.11: Operator Rolls the Die

If we go with the second option, we get

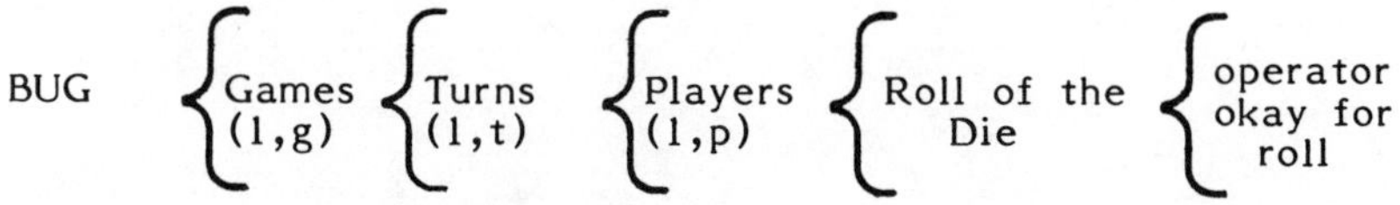

BUG { Games (1,g) { Turns (1,t) { Players (1,p) { Roll of the Die { operator okay for roll

Figure 6.12: Operator Okays Computer to Roll Die

This is the reason that for most computer games, there is only a very simple data base: the operator's response to go ahead with some action, or the operator's response to a question (like: Do you want to play another game, answer YES or NO).

## Review

Once more, let's go over the steps required to produce the Logical Data Base:

1. Remove the constant data elements (logical input structure)

2. Remove secondary data elements
3. Remove redundant data elements
4. Resolve all hidden hierarchies

These steps are also listed in the order in which they are normally used. It might also be pointed out that in the case that a Logical Output Structure has no secondary or redundant data elements or hidden hierarchies, then some or all of these steps may not be taken.

## EXERCISES

1. Complete the Logical Data Bases from the Logical Output Structures developed for Exercises 4.1 and 4.2.

# 7

# The Methodology: Physical Data Bases Part One

## EVENT ANALYSIS

### System Events

In our world, there are exceptions to just about every rule. Exceptions for this and for that occur in nearly all phases of our lives. Consequently, when doing computer processing with real-world data, some provisions must be made to handle the "special cases," or as some would say, the exceptions.

Traditionally, exception handling was done in a very haphazard and loose manner. Programmers would simply write their programs to handle the typical case, and then if any exception data was introduced to the program that made it fail, they would go back and patch up the program to handle that new exception. Consequently, programmers had to go back quite frequently to rewrite parts of their programs.

This approach to doing things is precisely what we need to get away from in the computer programming industry.

Consequently, with the Warnier-Orr program design methodology, we make the flat statement that there should be no exceptional data that is ever processed through our programs. Our programs should be able to process correctly all of the data that they can recognize, and they should be able to report and reject all data that they do not recognize. The programs should not go ahead and try to process data that they do not understand. This is one of the quickest ways in the world to make a program fail. Worst of all, to the casual observer the outputs will appear to be correct. And relying on incorrect results, as you can well understand, can be disastrous.

The techniques for handling the data once it is in the programs are also somewhat different. There is an age old argument that says that programs which are to read data files should be written so that they will work when there are no records in the file. This method of programming leads only to frustrated and paranoid programmers who write overly lengthy programs that check out every possible error condition that might occur. Writing a program with the assumption that there is at least one data record is the preferred technique--you just have to be sure that the program is never executed when there are no data records to process.

The same argument holds true for data that is being entered by an error-prone operator. A processing program should be written with the assumption that the data is error free; but there had better be a routine that verifies that all of the data is correct before that program is performed.

With these thoughts in mind, we are ready to plunge into the next major design phase for this technique. It is:

**STEP 3:** Define Events

This stage of the technique is known formally as event analysis. We begin with the Logical Data Base that we developed in the last chapter and begin to decompose it into different parts called entities and attributes. This is done to insure that the final product that we produce is correct, and that there are no data exceptions within the system.

## Entities

In the Logical Data Base, there are two types of data shown. The first of these types are called entities, and they show how different parts of the LDB relate to the other parts. Generally speaking, the entities of an LDB will be the names of the hierarchical brackets.

For our first examples of entities, let's examine the LDB for our savings account report of Figure 4.2, which is reproduced below:

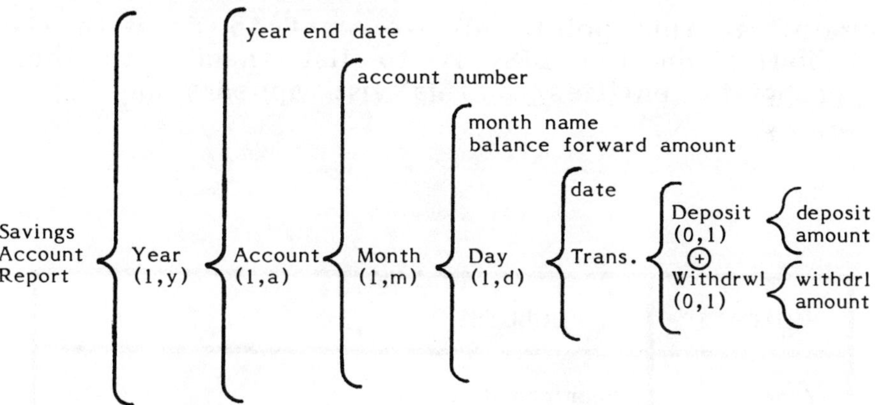


Figure 7.1: Report Logical Data Base

From this Logical Data Base, we will extract the names of all of the hierarchical brackets--the entities--and simply list them. This list appears in Figure 7.2.

## Attributes

As you might suspect, the attributes that we are speaking of in this section are also extracted from

Year
Account
Month
Day
Transaction
Deposit
Withdrawal

Figure 7.2: LDB Relationships

the Logical Data Base. Since the entities have all been gathered, the attributes are all of the data elements that are left on the LDB. Each of these attributes are associated with a particular entity. For example, the attribute year end date appears in the "Year" hierarchy; account number appears in the "Account" hierarchy; and so on.

Again, at this point, all we want to do with the attributes on the LDB is to list them with their appropriate entities. This list appears in Figure 7.3.

| ENTITY | ATTRIBUTES |
|---|---|
| Year | year end date |
| Account | account number |
| Month | month name; balance forward amount |
| Day | date |
| Transaction | ---- |
| Deposit | deposit amount |
| Withdrawal | withdrawal amount |

Figure 7.3 Relationships and Entities

## Events

Now that we have a list of all of the individual entities and their associated attributes, we need to do the actual definition of events stated in Step 3. We need to, for each of the entities listed, define all of the real-world events that can affect the attributes associated with it. For each of the entities, we need to:

1. Find out how a new entity can begin
2. Identify all events that can change attributes within an existing entity
3. Find out how an old entity can end

And, for each event that can change an entities' attributes, we must:

1. Identify which attributes will change
2. Identify how attributes will change

We do this event analysis once for each entity. This process, expressed in Warnier-Orr form, appears below.

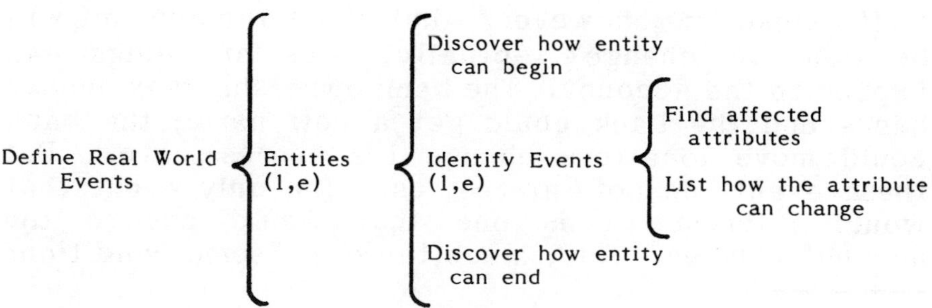


Figure 7.4: Definition of Events

This chart show the entire process for doing our event analysis.

So, for the list of entities and attributes of Figure 7.3, we proceed as directed. We start with the entity "Year."

How does a year begin? Well, you might say that a new year begins whenever the date changes from December 31 to January 1, and you would be correct for this example. But remember, not all years begin on January 1. Both the Jewish and the Chinese years do not begin on January 1, for example. But more closely tied to the business world, you will find that most fiscal years do not begin on January 1 either, and if you are doing fiscal year processing this is an important consideration.

As far as changes go, once a year has begun, it does not change until it is over (whenever on the calendar that occurs), so there are no events that will occur that will change the year number.* Therefore, we don't need to worry about having to change the year number once it is in the computer correctly.

For the entity "Account," we need to do the same analysis. An account can begin anytime that a new account is opened. The account will end whenever the account has been closed.

In the meantime, however, what about the account will be able to change? Actually, lot's of things can happen to the account. The bank ownership may change hands and the bank could get a new name; the bank could move locations change it's address; etc. But these events do not interest us. The only event that would interest us is one that would change the account number. And, since there are some conditions

---

* Actually, we should say that there are no likely events that could change the year number. The adoption of a different calendar would change the year number, but that event's chances of occuring are very small, and providing for that kind of a change is more trouble than it is worth.

under which our account could change numbers, we need to make a provision for that.

Or do we? If you have ever done much banking, you'll know that bankers do not like to change account numbers. This practice would leave them open to all sorts of bookkeeping errors that they'd just as soon not make. A bank would much rather close out an old account and open a different account for you with a new number. So really, there aren't any actions that can change an account number--just actions that can end an account.

For the entity "Month," the comments about the beginning and the ending of years are similarly applicable here, so we won't go any further into those. We do need to identify the events that could change either the balance forward amount or the month name. The month name is not likely to change, so we don't need to worry about that. And actually, there are only two events that could change the balance forward. One would be some sort of a bookkeeping error. And, if you have ever studied any accounting, you know that bookkeeping errors are never erased or removed--they must be reversed with another entry at the time that they are discovered. So, if an error was discovered in our balance forward amount, an adjusting entry would have to be inserted in our report. It could be a line which read:

```
          .
          .
          .
12    Balance Adjustment        12.31                    325.47
        Bank error
          .
          .
```

Figure 7.5: Adjusting Entry

The other thing that could affect the balance forward amount, is a little thing known as interest. Since banks periodically pay interest on the money saved in their account, this means that your account balance will go up occasionally without your having made a deposit. However, this is still a deposit and could be handled as if it were a normal deposit transaction. So this change does not require anything new.

But the bookeeping entry does require something new. Since this is a new entry, only discovered during this analysis, we will need to go back and adjust all of the work that we have done up until now. We need to add the bookeeping entry to our sample output, our Logical Output Structure, and our Logical Data Base. The bookkeeping entry becomes a new transaction, and it is added to the LDB like this:

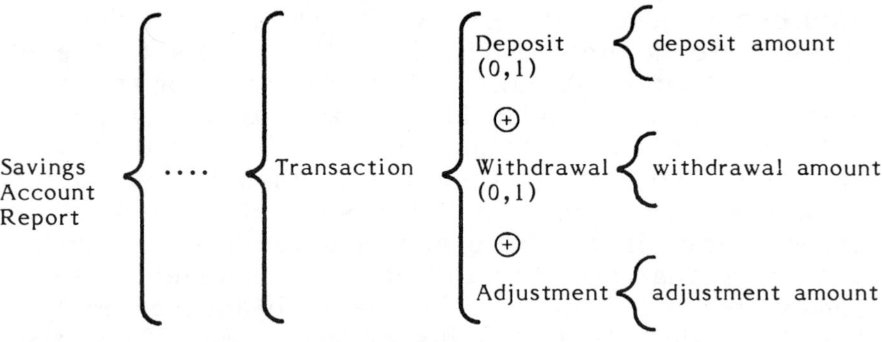


Figure 7.6: Addition to Logical Data Base

We also get a new entity and attribute to consider:

| ENTITY | ATTRIBUTE |
|---|---|
| Adjustment | adjustment amount |

Figure 7.7: New Relationship and Entity

You might also notice that since the adjustment could be either a credit to the account or a debit to the account, the adjustment amount will have to be a signed amount--either positive (for a debit) or negative (for a credit). This characteristic is carried with the number as it is stored in the computer and does not require a separate positive/negative indicator for the transaction.

For the "Day" entity, the comments for the "Month" and the "Year" entities both apply.

For Transactions, there are no events to consider, since there are no attributes that may be changed.

For each of the transactions, "Deposit," "Withdrawal," and now "Adjustment," the same comments will apply, so we'll not examine each of them individually. Each of the transactions will begin whenever they occur, and, once they have occurred, they do not end. This is a characteristic that we have not seen before. Also, for each transaction, the only way that the amount associated with it may change is if it is found to be in error. And, since this just requires another adjusting transaction to rectify, we need not be concerned with it.

So now we have completed the primary event analysis for this process. Since this is such a lengthy process, we won't go into the details for the other outputs that we have been following. Just some general comments will suffice.

### Common Events

There are some common occurrences that justify doing the event analysis at this time. One of them was pointed out in the example that was worked through: you may discover additional requirements for the output that were previously unknown. Also, you may find that you need to incorporate the facility to change some of the attributes once they are correctly in the computer. And, although we did not see any need to do that in the example that we worked, this is a more common occurrence.

For instance, take the example of a report which included information about the entity "Customer."

Typically, customers have numbers used within an organization to uniquely identify them. But they also have names, addresses and telephone numbers, all of which may change at any time without changing the actual identity of the customer. You would not want to go through the process for removing an old customer from your records and adding a new one every time that a customer moved, or got married, or had their phone number changed. You would instead want to be able to alter the old data in the computer, and would want to design your processes with that facility in mind.

## EXERCISES

1. Do an event analysis for the two other reports and the BUG game covered in the previous chapters.

2. Do an event analysis for each of the problems given at the end of Chapter 4.

# 8

# The Methodology: Physical Data Bases Part Two

## PHYSICAL DESIGN

### Physical Considerations

So far in this book, we have included very little in the way of "real world" examples, i.e., physical representations of designed structures. This was intentional. In fact, until after you have completed the Logical Data Base for a design and a detailed event analysis, physical considerations should be totally and exactly zero. You must design the logic of an application before you can even consider any of the possible physical realizations of it. The lesson that taught us this was learned only after many years of hard experience.

The reason that physical considerations are postponed until this point are twofold. First of all, considering the physical aspects of the application too soon will bring on all kinds of problems. We begin to worry whether or not a logical design will be possible to implement on the equipment that we have available and then begin to change the design. We worry if the machine that we have will execute the routines quickly enough; whether there will be enough storage to do the job; whether the data should be kept in the computer or on magnetic tape; whether a given set of data should be stored as a file or an in-core table and so on.

Actually, you'll find that this sort of designing/ worrying will only give you ulcers and chewed fingernails, not results. Up until this point in the design phase, you simply don't know enough about the problem to be concerned with physical limitations.

Secondly, there is a maintenance problem to consider. So far, this has not been a big problem for microcomputer users. But there will come a time when you'll want to change your system over from a small, paper tape oriented system to a larger, magnetic tape or disk operated system. Later, you'll probably change from an 8-bit microcomputer to a 16-bit micro. Eventually, you may even find yourself drooling over the latest 32-bit microcomputer (which is sort of a contradiction of terms) with a bubble memory operating system. Each of these steps upward in hardware will necessitate a formidable change in software.

If you have designed your software correctly, then you will have a sound, logical and correct design for your problems, and implementation on a different machine configuration becomes so simple that it is almost trivial. Conversion, instead of taking months, is now only a matter of a few days, with much less hair-pulling and teeth-gnashing.

You can see that if we designed our programs to only work on one type of machine, conversion to another would be at best very difficult and at worst downright impossible. This is always the case.

Designing with physical considerations too soon can bring you all kinds of sorrow and grief. Take for instance, the predicament that one state government found itself in a few years ago. It seems that this state owned a certain type of disk storage unit on which they stored all of their drivers license information. Each of the individual drivers license numbers corresponded to a physical area on the disk. Thus, when motor vehicles wanted to know the information that belonged to the drivers license number "A1M5F9" they simply fed that number into their computer and it looked up the disk address "A1M5F9" and got the information that they needed. Pretty slick, right? Wrong. You can imagine their difficulty when the next generation of machines came out. None of the new disk packs were addressed that way, and, since the old license numbers were entered on a first come, first serve basis and not alphabetically, changing them over to a new machine was a treacherous task indeed. It was so difficult in fact, that they delayed changing to a new computer for several years for that very reason. Finally, they were forced to convert to a new machine, but they had to completely overhaul their drivers license operation at great expense and considerable time.

If they had built their design on a logical basis instead of a physical basis, their conversion would have been a relatively simple matter. They would not have had to put off acquiring a newer and faster machine that was badly needed. They would have been in much better shape all around, if they had only designed logically instead of physically.

Magic numbers--those numbers used in the computer to represent two or more different things at the same time--are found in similar systems all over the world today. And the more different meanings that a magic number has, the harder it is to change, for whatever reason that the change needs to occur. In the end, those magic numbers usually result in a complete redesign of the entire system that they are in, since it eventually becomes impossible to change anything.

**Physical Data Base**

The next phase in the Warnier-Orr design technique requires that we for our application. The Physical Data Base is the physical realization of the Logical Data Base which we have just finished. It is the way that the data that we keep in our computer will actually be arranged.

## Files

The concept of a file is not a new one. Everyone is familiar with some sort of a file cabinet that has drawers full of file folders. In the computer industry, the concept of a file is exactly the same. A file is a collection of individual records, where each record contains the same kinds of information. Not the same information, but the same kinds of information. For instance, a customer file will have many records, each of which will contain information about one customer. The records could contain things like the customer's name, the customer's address, the customer's telephone number, etc. Each record will contain the above information, but individual entries will be unique for each customer.

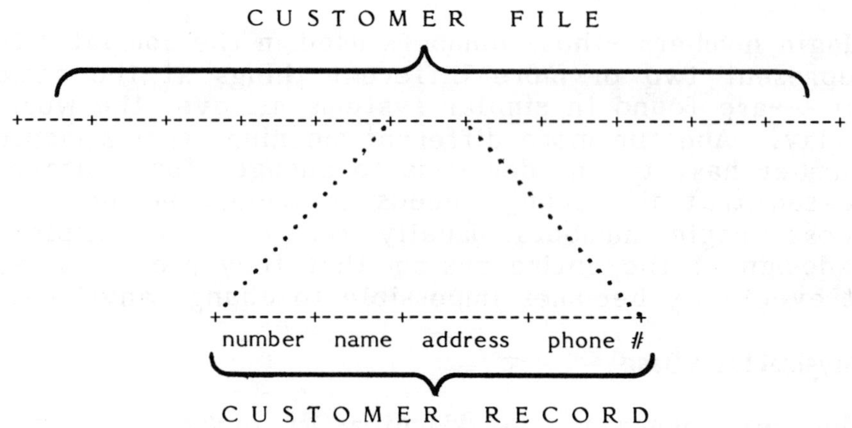


Figure 8.1: Files and Records

Files can be imagined as being a string of areas stored in the computer. Each one of those areas is where the individual information is kept are the records.

So what we are actually going to be designing in this phase are files, each one of which is going to contain some records.

## File Layout

In order to get some sort of a feel for actually laying out the physical arrangement of the Logical Data Base, let's return to the savings account report. If you'll remember back to Chapter 4, we said that to produce that savings account activity report by hand, we would want all of our financial records in one place and sorted by account, month, and day. Then we would have all of the information in the order in which we need to use it.

But just what kind of information would we want to have on those sorted records? Obviously, we want to include as many of the reports' primary data elements on these records, so let's just go down the list of the elements on our Logical Data Base.

The first primary data element, the "year end date," doesn't seem to be something that we'd want to keep on each and every one of our records; after all, we only need it once: at the beginning of the report. Keeping the year end date on each and every one of our transaction records would be an enormous waste of space in the file. Therefore, we'll keep the year end date somewhere else in the computer, where we can look it up at the beginning of the report.

We would however, want to keep the "account number," the "month name" and the "date." We represent a record with this infomation on it with the use of "data buckets" (└──────┘) which indicate an area on the record in which the data element can be found. So far on our record, we have

⌊account number⌋ ⌊month name⌋ ⌊day⌋ . . . . .

Figure 8.2: Partial Data Record

But we also would want to keep the amount of the deposit, the withdrawal, or the adjustment for that day on the record. We could do it with three large data buckets; one for a deposit amount, one for a withdrawal amount, and one for an adjustment amount. But, since only one amount is ever going to be present on any one record, we really only need one large bucket to hold an amount, and one small bucket to indicate whether the amount is a deposit, a withdrawal, or an adjustment. This saves us some space on the record, because the deposit/withdrawal/ adjustment indicator will only take up one character of room (it will be either a "D," a "W," or an "A") while the other amount fields would take up seven or eight characters apiece. We traditionally call this type of field a "transaction code" or a "transaction type."

One more data element that we need to consider is the "balance forward" for each month. For the month of January, the balance forward is the balance of the account going into the year, which is a primary data element. However, for each month after that, the balance forward is a computed element; the current balance at the end of the previous month becomes the next months' balance forward.

Since it seems that we only need to find out the balance forward only once at the beginning of each account, it sounds like we would not want to keep an area for it on each one of our records. Keeping it there would waste an incredible amount of room, as the space that it would occupy would only have an amount in it once at the beginning of each account. The rest of the time, that area of the record would be unused and ignored.

It would be much better if we could look up the

beginning balance for each account on a separate record once at the beginning of each account. If we do keep the balance forward in a different place, then the data record we have built looks like:

account number | month name | date | trans.type | amount

Figure 8.3: Complete Data Record

If we had this information on our records, had the records sorted in the right order, and had the "year "end date" and the account "balances forward," then we would be able to successfully produce the Savings Account Activity report. By a strange coincidence (actually it's not strange at all), if we eliminate from our Logical Data Base the elements "year end

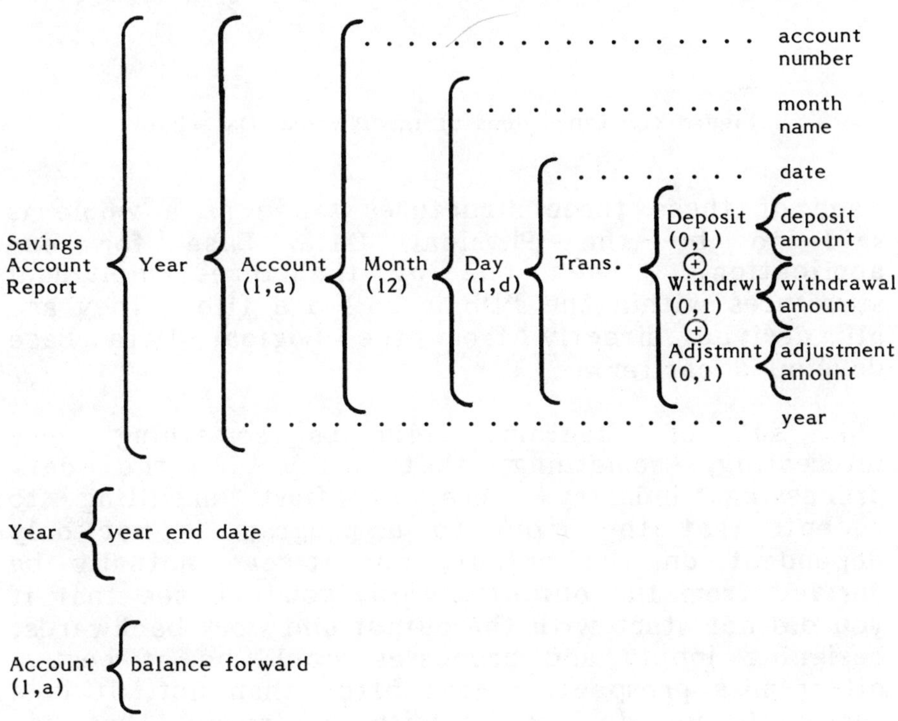


Figure 8.4: Physical Data Base

date" and "balance forward," put them in a separate place with their associated entities, and the shove the remaining data elements over to the right on the diagram, we get a large diagram which mirrors exactly the record that we just constructed.

All of the elements left on the structure, when read from top to bottom, describe exactly the record that we decided we needed. The structure, in turn, describes the sort sequence that we want our records in.

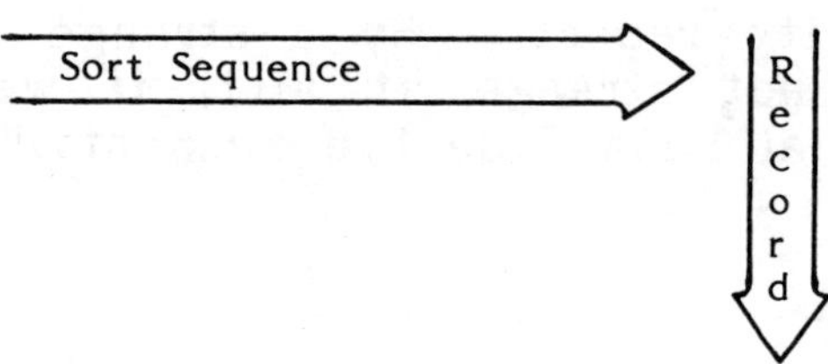


Figure 8.5: Dimensions of the Physical Data Base

Each of those three structures taken as a whole is said to be the Physical Data Base for our application. Each one of the three individual structures within the PDB is called a file. They are all derived directly from the Logical Data Base developed earlier.

This set of diagrams tells us something very interesting; something that many in the data processing industry were at first unwilling to accept: that the input to a program is not only dependent on the output, but it can actually be derived from the output! Again, you can see that if you did not start with the output and work backwards, designing inputs and processes would be at best a hit-or-miss prospect. More often than not, it is a miss. If you don't start with the output that you want, trying to guess what input that you'll need is simply ridiculous.

Once more, let's go over the process that we used to design the Physical Data Base:

1. Begin with the Logical Data Base
2. Eliminate once or twice per program primary data elements: put them in a separate record grouped by their associated entity
3. List the data elements from top to bottom for each of the physical files produced to obtain the data record

What you will end up with is a diagram that will tell you the information you need to have on your input records and the order that those records must be in to produce the correct output.

## Previously Defined Inputs

For most microcomputer applications, the above method of designing a Physical Data Base will suffice. However, there is one assumption made here that may not always be valid with respect to program design: the input for your program may have been previously defined.

In the data processing industry, this is more the rule than the exception. Most systems which are already in operation will have the data that you will want to use already captured: the only problem is that it may not be sorted in the sequence in which you need it, and the information that you want could be spread out over many different records on a dozen different files. What happens then?

In cases like these, where the data is already defined and is not in the form that you need, then you'll have to do a bit more work. Those files that were developed that together make up the Physical Data Base will become ideal files. Ideal simply means that if you had your way, that is what your input files would look like. All that you need to do then is to build a front end program which translates the already defined files that are available into files which you can use. This makes your program a two-step process--one which assembles data into a form which you can use (your ideal files) and one which actually processes that data.

## Other Physical Data Bases

You've now seen the process for deriving the Physical Data Base as it applies to a hierarchical report. The process is precisely the same for other reports.

Let's see what the Physical Data Base is for the game of "BUG" discussed earlier. If we look again at the second Logical Data Base for the game

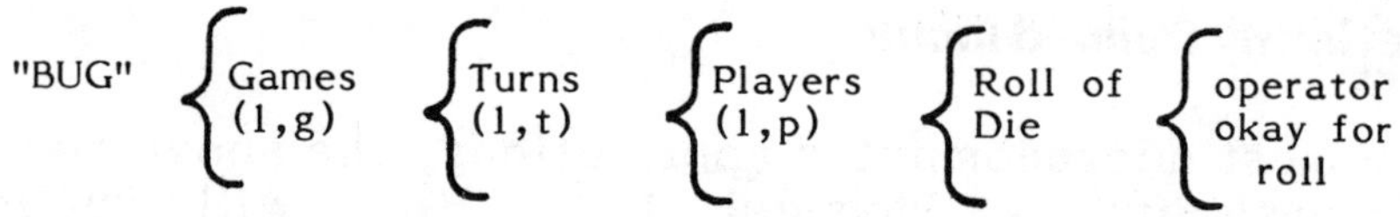

"BUG" { Games (1,g) { Turns (1,t) { Players (1,p) { Roll of Die { operator okay for roll

Figure 8.6: "BUG" Logical Data Base

we'll find that the Physical Data Base is precisely the same. It consists of a single logical record which will hold the operator okay for the next roll of the die.

It is for this reason that for many microcomputer programs, the time spent in the analysis of the Logical and Physical Data Bases will be very small. However, no matter how small the Logical and Physical Data Bases turn out to be, they still exist for every application and they remain important steps in the program design work.

## EXERCISES

1. Finish the Physical Data Bases for the two other reports developed in Chapters 5 and 6.

2. Do the Physical Data Bases For the projects at the end of Chapter 4.

# 9

# The Methodology:
## Logical Process Design

### Tying It All Together

Through the last five chapters, we have managed to describe a fixed process by which anyone can take an output that is wanted and produce from it the correct inputs needed and the order that they need to be in. About the only thing left to find out for a process is how to take those inputs, now that we know what they are and what they look like, and describe a procedure for converting this ideal input into the correct output that we need.

The use of the Warnier-Orr diagram is particularly valuable in this aspect of the design. Throughout this step we will build on all of the work that we have done up until now to produce a "logical program blueprint" from which we can directly code a program.

**STEP 5:** Design the Logical Process

In order to design the logical process, we must begin back at the original data structure that was developed for a problem. Of course, this structure may have changed somewhat since it was done originally. Because of the event analysis, there may now be a previously hidden hierarchy or an unknown requirement which we can add to the data structure. All new information that has been discovered about the system must be integrated at this point into the old diagrams. For instance, the data structure for our savings account report example has changed a bit. The data structure as it now looks appears in Figure 9.1.

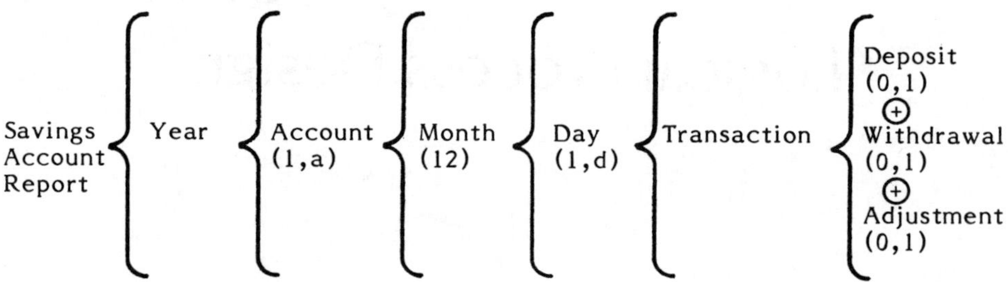


Figure 9.1: Updated Data Structure

We've incorporated into the data structure the change necessitated by the discovery of the requirement of an adjustment transaction.

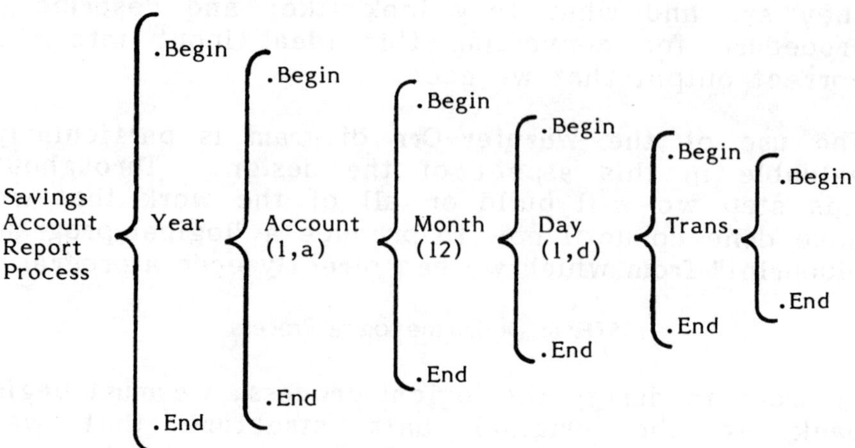


Figure 9.2: Data Structure Detail

Now we are ready to begin the procedure of describing the logical process. You'll recall we said earlier that large processes can always be broken up into at least three steps; a beginning, a middle, and an end. This is what we will first do to every level of our data structure, except for the lowest level. The lowest level will be completed later in the chapter.

The ".Begin" and the ".End" that was added to each level of the hierarchy segments each level into the three elementary parts. The dot preceding the word is just a shorthand way of indicating a carry-over of the name of that particular level. Thus, at the Year level

Year { .Begin
.End }

the ".Begin" is to be read "Year Begin" or "Begin Year," whichever you prefer, and the ".End" is to be read "Year End" or "End Year."

With this compartmentalization done, we can now begin to fill in the details of the process, which is

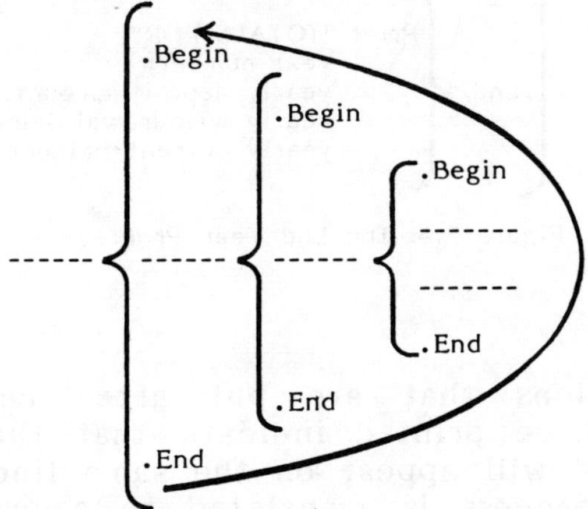


Figure 9.3: Direction of Process Completion

called the "definition of elementary mappings." We fill these compartments from the bottom to the top--from the ".End" of the highest level to the process to the ".Begin" of the higest level of the process. The arrow on the diagram of Figure 9.3 shows the order in which we fill in the details of the diagram.

So, for the savings account report, we first need to fill in the "End Savings Account Report Process" bracket. To do this, we need to examine the Logical Output Structure and decide what action must take place to procuce the required outputs. In this case, we find that there are no outputs that need to be produced at the end of the Report Process, so we leave that bracket empty for the time being.

Next, we move on up to the "End Year" bracket. Looking at the LOS, we see that there are some totals that need to get printed at this time. So, that is what we need to indicate on our process.

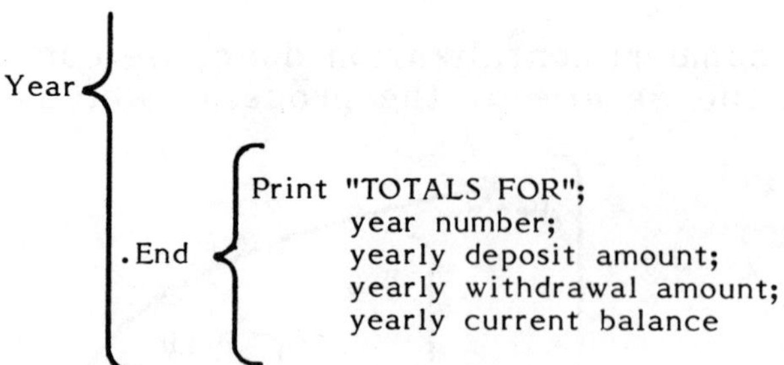


Figure 9.4: The End Year Process

The semicolons that are put after each of the elements to be printed indicate that the following field printed will appear on the same line. So that when this process is translated to a program, the line that will actually be printed is:

TOTALS FOR 1977 2,345.67 4,567.89 211.13

instead of:

TOTALS FOR
1977
2,345.67
4,567.89
211.13

The absence of the semicolon after the "yearly current balance" element indicates that it is the last entry on that particular line, and that the next element printed will begin on the following line.

The next bracket to fill in will be the "End Account." Again looking at the LOS, we find that there is some output to be printed here. There is also another matter to attend to at this time--and that is the summation of the account totals to form the yearly totals. You can see that the sum totals of all of the individual accounts will produce the yearly totals. So that if, at the end of each account, we add that accounts totals to the yearly

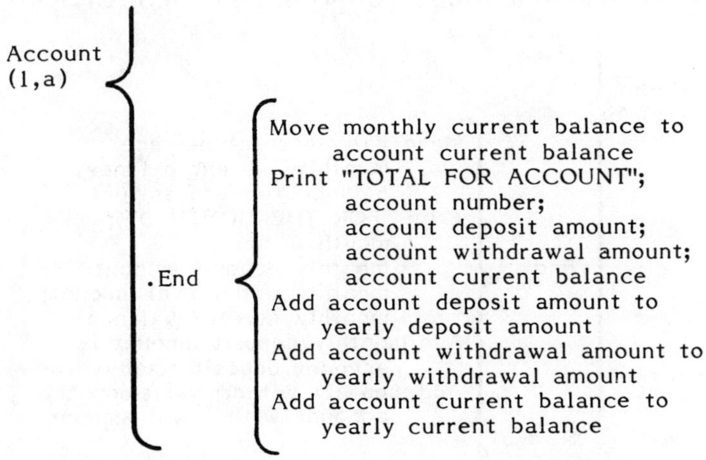


Figure 9.5: End Account Process

totals, we will have the correct figure to print when we are done with the year. We also need to find the value of the last "monthly current balance" to print as the "account current balance."

Notice that we are going into great detail in these processes. Each action that is to be performed is explicitly spelled out. Once you get used to the diagrams and become more and more familiar with their operation, a lot of this minute detail can be implied. The two sentences:

Print Account Totals
Add Account Totals to the Yearly Totals

would probably be sufficient detail for the "End Account" process. However, for now let's break out the processes to their final detail.

Moving on up the diagram, we next take care of the "End Month" process. Again, as with the end of the Account process, we need to print the monthly totals and add the monthly totals to the account totals. Also, we need to get the last daily current balance and use it for the monthly current balance and the balance forward amount for the next month.

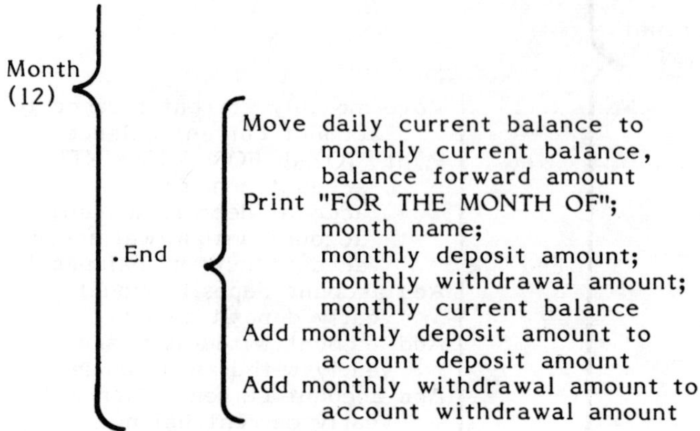


Figure 9.6: End Month Process

Notice that we did not add the monthly current balance to the account current balance. If you look at the sample output, you'll see that the account current balance is not the sum of all of the monthly current balances. It is instead, simply the last monthly current balance amount printed again. So summing this result would be incorrect.

Next, at the "End Day" process, we only need to print the daily current balance figure.

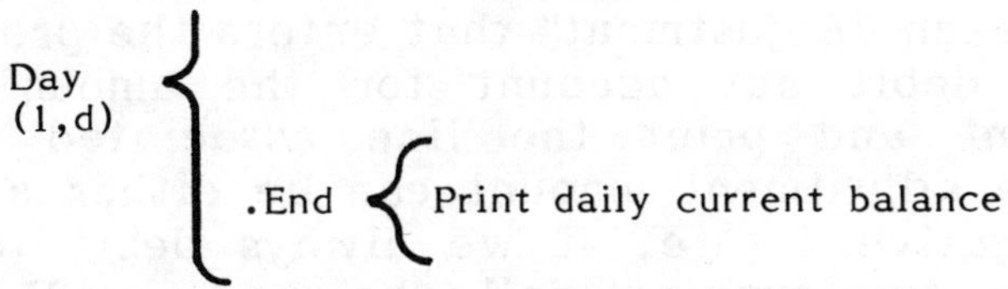


Figure 9.7: End Day Process

And at the "End Transaction" process, there is apparently no action that need to take place. Actually, one of the most important steps of the process will occur here, but we'll talk more about that later on. For now, we leave the bracket empty.

We are now down to this point in our data structure

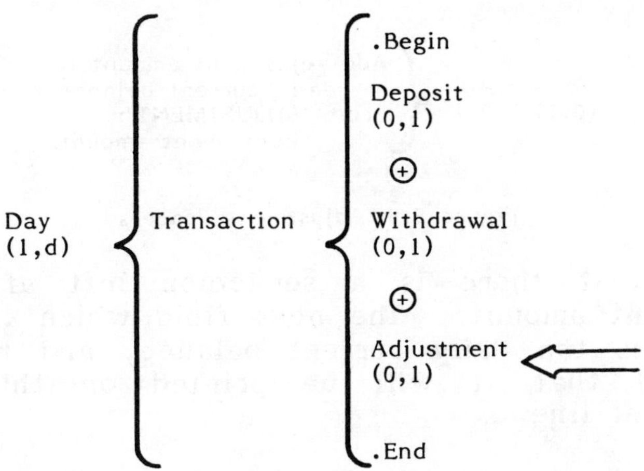


Figure 9.8: Next Bracket to Complete

We said earlier that the lowest level brackets were not broken down into ".Begin" and ".End" compartments. Since there is no "middle" of any of these processes (that is, none of them break down into another level of hierarchy), the beginning and the ending are always performed one right after the other, and usually they are simple enough that we do not need to break them apart into two separate processes. We leave them as a single process that is performed one time.

So, for each "Adjustment" that enters the process, we need to debit out account for the amount of the adjustment and print the line associated with it. Since the adjustment amount can be either a positive or a negative figure, if we always debit (add) the figure to the running daily balance, we'll get the correct result. Adding a negative amount is the same as subtracting a positive amount. This means that all of the adjustments which are negative will print as negative debits instead of positive credits. We could write the program to check the adjustment amount and then print it as a positive credit to the account if the figure were negative, but for the moment we'll be content to leave it as a positive or negative debit.

```
Adjustment  { Add adjustment amount to
(0,1)       {     daily current balance
            { Print "ADJUSTMENT";
            {         adjustment amount;
```

Figure 9.9: Adjustment Process

Notice that there is a semicolon left after the adjustment amount. The next field which is to be printed is the daily current balance, and we have indicated that it will be printed on this same adjustment line.

The processes for both the "Deposit" and the "Withdrawal" transactions are essentially the same as for the "Adjustment." The daily current balance must be updated and the transaction line needs to be printed. These processes appear in Figures 9.10 and 9.11.

```
               ┌ Subtract withdrawal amount from
Withdrawal     │     daily current balance
(0,1)          │ Print "WITHDRAWAL";
               └     withdrawal amount;
```

Figure 9.10: Withdrawal Process

```
               ┌ Add deposit amount to
Deposit        │      daily current balance
(0,1)          │ Print "DEPOSIT";
               └      deposit amount;
```

Figure 9.11: Deposit Process

Now we move on up to our first ".Begin" bracket-- the "Begin Transaction" process. Before we get into the process, though, there is a small matter to explain.

## Data Areas

Back in Chapter 6, we talked briefly about the "logical pigeon holes" in the computer where our numbers were stored. Those locations which hold our numbers must be carefully maintained by our programs. We need to empty the location before we ever use it to clear out any old numbers which might still be in the location from a previous program, and we need to empty the location each time we need start a new calculation with it. Therefore, one of the things that must be done at each one of the ".Begin" processes is to clear out the "logical pigeon holes" which that level of the program will use. This action is known as initializing program variables.

Now, getting back to our diagram, in the "Begin Transaction" process, there are apparently no actions that need to take place. There are no transaction summation areas that should be cleared. So we leave this bracket empty.

The next bracket to be filled in, the "Begin Day" bracket, has no summation fields to clear, but it does have an output to print.

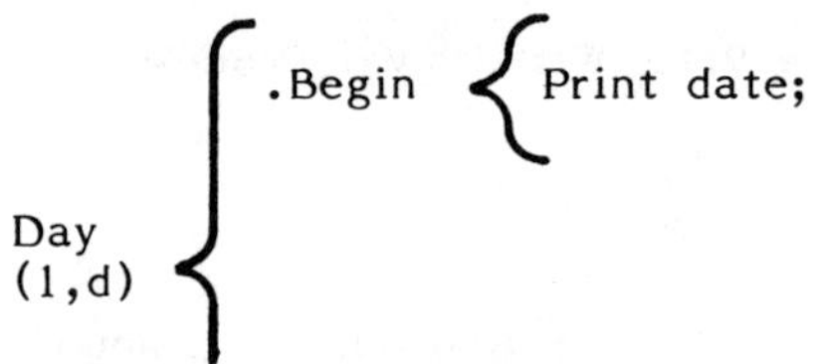


Figure 9.12: Begin Day Process

The next process to be completed is the "Begin Month" process. It does have some summation fields that need to be initialized, and there is also some output that needs to be printed.

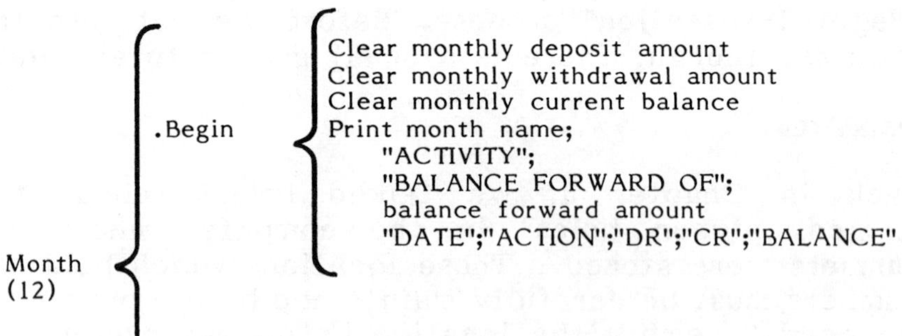


Figure 9.13: Begin Month Process

Next, we move up to the "Begin Account" process, which appears in Figure 9.14.

Notice that some of the design considerations from our Physical Data Base show up at this point. Since the monthly current balance is a primary data element for the month of January (the beginning of each new account) and is then a computed element for the rest

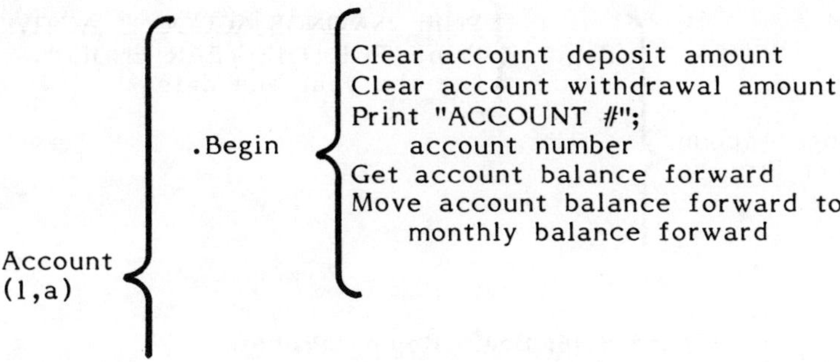


Figure 9.14: Begin Account Process

of the months, we go get the first balance at the beginning of each account, and then for each subsequent month, we save the previous month's current balance as the next month's balance forward. That part of the process occurs in the "End Month" routine.

Now, we need to fill in the "Begin Year" process.

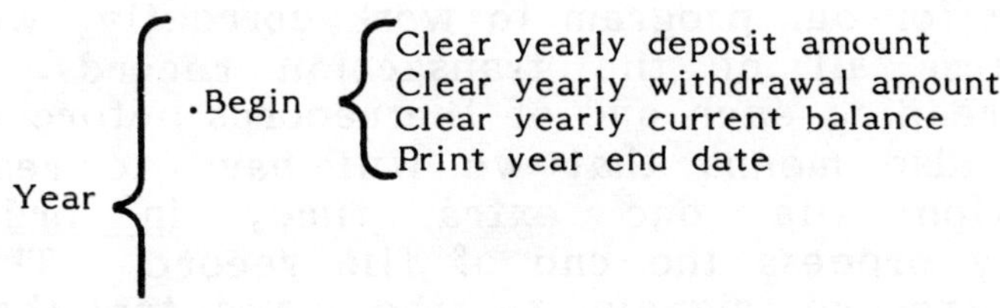


Figure 9.15: Begin Year Process

And we need to fill in the final bracket, "Begin Report," as in Figure 9.16

There is also something else which needs to be done in this process, and it is related to the thing that we said should be done in the "End Transaction" process earlier. The time has come to address that subject.

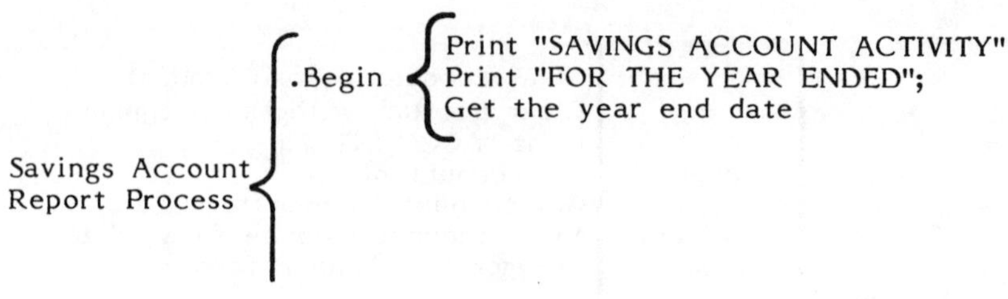


Figure 9.16: Begin Report Process

## Reading Records

Remember that this particular program is going to process some files. One of those files will contain only one record--the year end date. The other file will contain several records--one for each account--and each record will have on it the account balance forward. We'll also have a transaction file, and each record of that file will describe one transaction.

In order for our program to work correctly, we need to process all of the transaction records. This entails reading each one of the records before we use it. It also means that we will have to read the transaction file one extra time, in order to correctly process the end of file record. This end of file record signals to the computer that the supply of transaction records has been exhausted and that there are no more records left to read. So all in all, when we are finished with the program, if there were "t" transaction records, then we will have read the transaction file "t+1" times.

This is important to know, because that means that the read statements in our program must be placed somewhere where they will be executed "t+1" times. The proper way to do that then, is to place one read statement in the "End Transaction" process, since the "End Transaction" process will be executed exactly "t" times. That leaves us with one extra read which we must place in the "Begin Report" process, since it is only executed one time. This will give us our "t+1" reads. It also allows us to remain one record ahead of ourselves all of the time in the program, so that we may properly end the heirarchical levels at the appropriate time. We'll discuss this more in the next chapter, which is about physical design considerations.

For now, we have completed the logical design for this report program. We have an accurate and complete logical program blueprint. However, there are still some things that we'll need to add to this design if it is to actually be implemented on a computer. We must consider some physical characteristics of computers before the design can be complete.

## The BUG Program

Let's look at the design process for the BUG game that we have been developing. Again, let's start with the basic structure of the game.

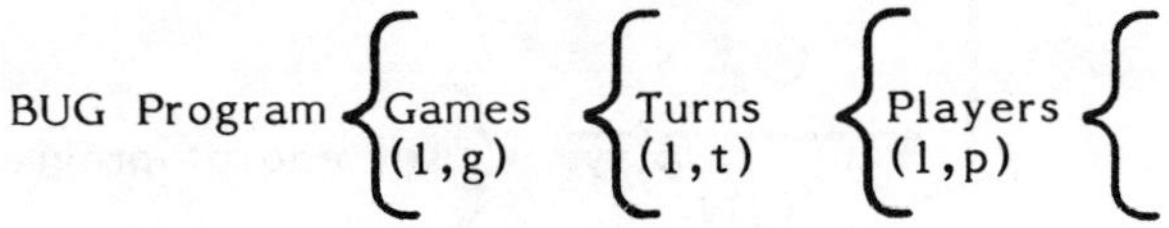

BUG Program { Games (1,g) { Turns (1,t) { Players (1,p) {

Figure 9.17: Bug Program Structure

Again, we'll compartmentalize the structure and fill in the needed processes from bottom to top. Therefore, the first bracket to fill will be "Program.End." About the only thing to do in this bracket is to have the computer say goodbye to the human player. This is shown in Figure 9.18.

The next compartment to fill is the "Game.End" process. At the end of the game, we'll first declare the winner of the game and then ask the human player if he wants to play another game. If he does, we'll

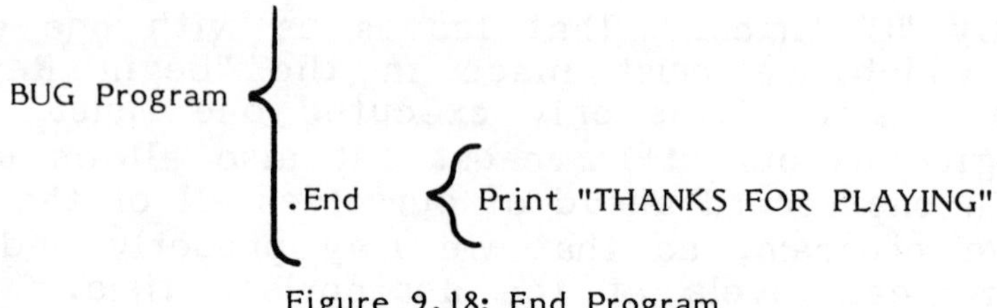


Figure 9.18: End Program

go back and start a new game. Otherwise, we'll fall through to the "Program.End" process.

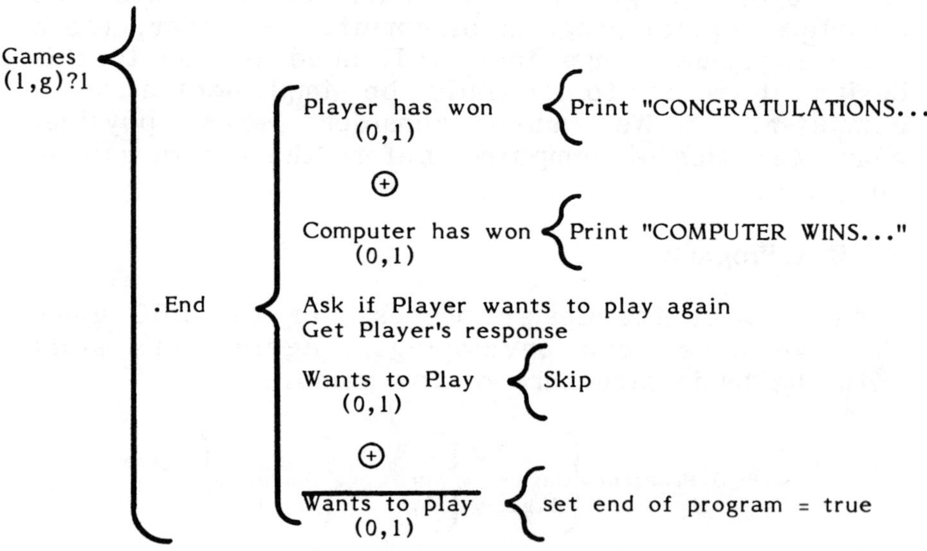


NOTES:
?1 - end of program = true

Figure 9.19: End Game

Notice that the "Games" process is repeated again and again until the end of program indicator is set equal to true. Thus, when the player indicates that he does not want to play another game, the "Games" process will be terminated and we will fall through to the "Program.End" process.

Next, we define the process for the end of a turn.

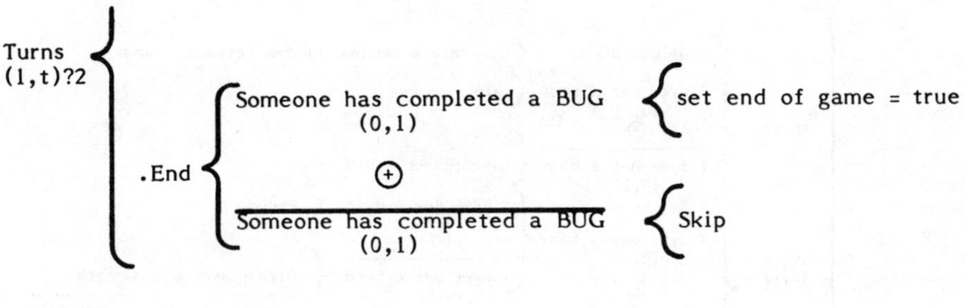


Figure 9.20: End Turn

We are going to do something a little different with the next level. Since we only have two players, the computer and the human opponent, we can separate them at the "Turn" level like this:

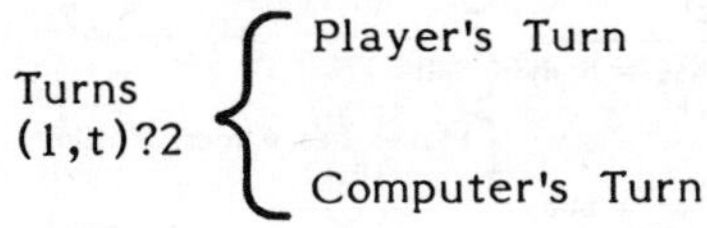


Figure 9.21 - Decision process for each roll of die

During each one to the turns, we need to have the computer roll the dice (generate a random number between 1 and 6) and then decide if the participant gets that part of the BUG. Since the decision process is the same for both participants, we'll only develop it once.

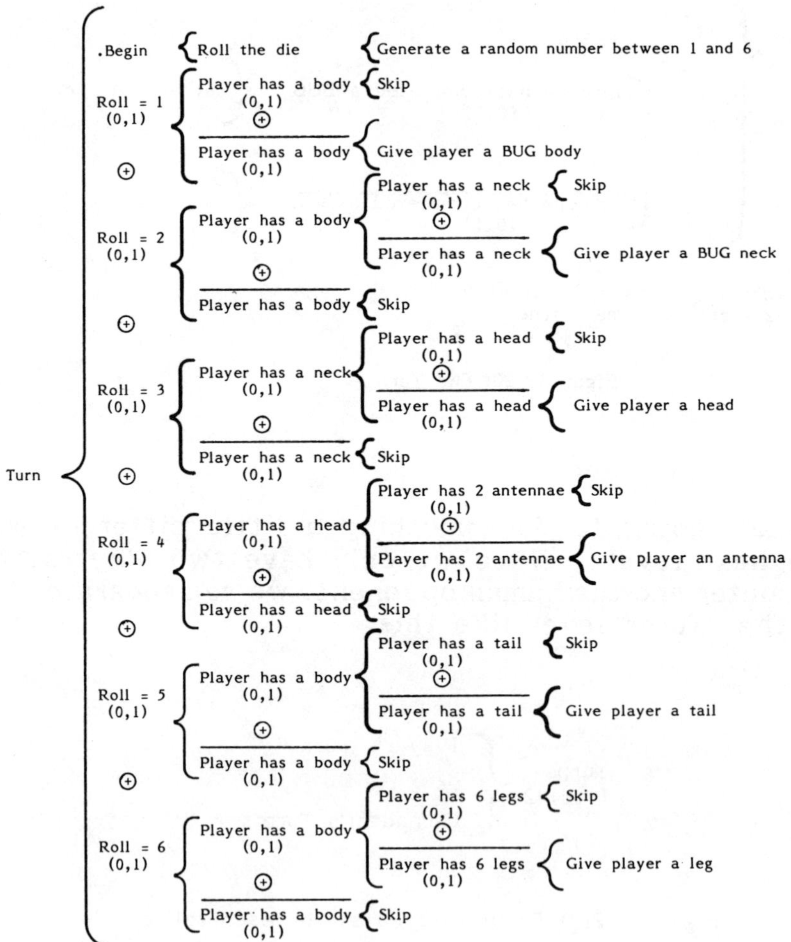


Figure 9.21: Decision Process for Each Turn

Then, the only things which remain are the "Game.Begin" process, where we initialize the BUG parts for the players, and the "Program.Begin" process, where we explain the rules to the player. We also need to set the end of game indicator and the end of program indicator so those processes get executed properly.

The finished diagram of the BUG program appears in Figure 9.23.

## EXERCISES

Complete the logical design for either one of the report programs discussed earlier or for one of the exercise programs from the previous chapters.

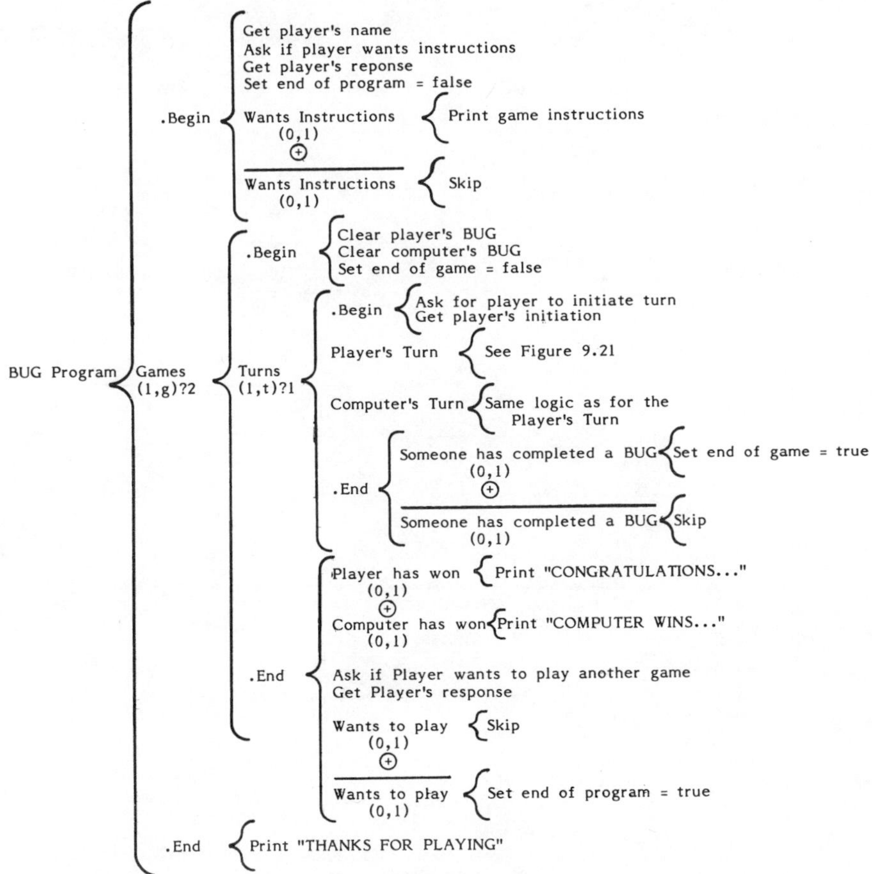


Figure 9.22: Bug Program Design

# 10

# The Methodology: Physical Design

## Physical Considerations

We have come to the last step in our program design methodology. Up to this point, we have developed the output for our program, its Data Structure, its Logical Data Base, its Physical Data Base, and its logical design. The only thing that we need to do, after having completed the logical design for our problem, is to take into consideration some physical characteristics of computers in general.

This last step of the program design phase is:

**STEP 6:** Design the Physical Process

The two primary things we will be concerned with in this phase are called control breaks and some special file handling procedures.

## Control Breaks

On our logical process diagram, we have charted the time and the place for all of the activities that must occur to produce the correct output. What we have not yet considered is the problem of getting the hierarchical cycles represented to actually work in computer program form. Logically, that is not a problem, because we assume at some point the program will be able to tell, for instance, when it is at the end of an account or the end of a day. However, when we actually turn this design into a computer program, we need to set up the routines to make sure that those control breaks do indeed occur at the proper times. Therefore, this is a physical consideration of our design and not a logical one.

So how are the control breaks set up for a program like this. Well, let's first consider how a person producing this report by hand would recognize the breaks. Let's actually go through the logical design that we developed in the last chapter.

The first time that we start down the logical process, we'll perform all of the ".Begin" processes. First, we pick up the starting transaction record from our file and then go through the action of initializing in turn all of the different report level totals. We perform the processes in this order:

```
Savings Account Report
    Begin Report
    Year
        Begin Year
        Account
            Begin Account
            Month
                Begin Month
                Day
                    Begin Day
                    Transaction
                        Begin Transaction
                                .
                                .
```

Figure 10.1: Execution of the Logical Design

Then, depending on whether the transaction is a deposit, a withdrawal, or an adjustment, we'll perform one of those three processes. Say that the first transaction is a deposit. We peform the process for a deposit and then perform the "End Transaction" routine, where we are instructed to get the next transaction record.

But now what? Do we fall through the bracket and perform the "End Day" process? Or do we continue to stay in the "Transaction" phase and go back to the "Begin Transaction" process again?

If the possibility exists that there could be more than one transaction for a single day (an assumption which we have not made yet) then we need to find out if this new transaction occurred on the same day as the last transaction. If it did, then we remain in the "Transaction" process and do not leave it until, sometime in the future, we run across a transaction record which did not occur on the same day. To assume that there can be multiple transactions on a single day requires that we add the following notation to our logical design.

Transaction {
(1,t)

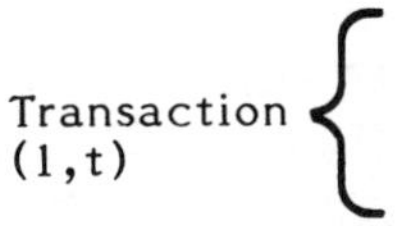

Figure 10.2: New Requirement

So we see that if the transaction on the next record occured on the same date as the transation before it, then we stay in a loop in the program--we repeat the process "Transaction" until such time that we run across a new transaction date.

This process, of comparing an attribute of a previous record with the same attribute of the next record to see if they are the same, will require an additional modification to our logical design. We need to be able to have the program "remember" the old attribute. So we must, at some point, save the old attribute for comparing, and use the results of our comparison to either continue the repetitive process that we are in or to terminate it and fall through to the next process.

To illustrate the concept further, look at the structured narrative shown in Figure 10.3. This narrative tells us that before we do the repetitive process, we must save the current transaction date and set an indicator called "End of Transactions" false. It will ultimately be the truth or fallacy of this indicator which will determine whether or not to continue the repetition.

```
Let old transaction date be the current transaction date.
Set "End of Transactions" False.
Do, until "End of Transactions" is True:
      Begin Transaction,
      either Deposit,
      or Withdrawal,
      or Adjustment,
      End Transaction:
          get next record,
          If transaction date is not the
              same as old transaction date
              then set "End of Transactions" True.
End Do.
```

Figure 10.3: Narrative of Physical Control Break

Examination of this narrative will show that we'll need to save the transaction date and set the control break indicator false before we perform the "Transaction" process. So we'll add these two instructions to the "Begin Day" process--the last process to be executed before the "Transaction" process begins.

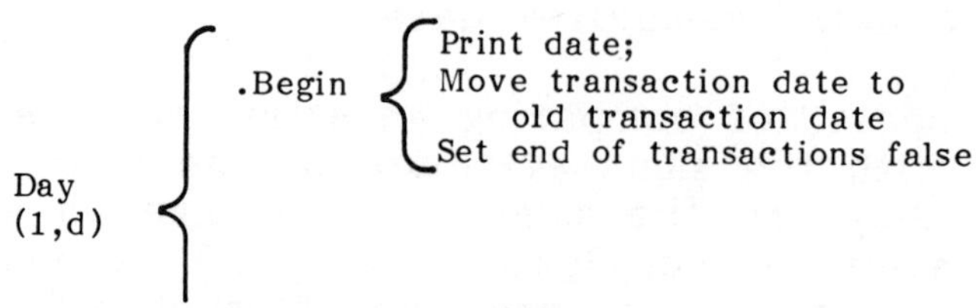


Figure 10.4: Addition to the Begin Day Process

However, we do not add the test for the end of transaction to the "End Transaction" process. This test is an implied test which is inherent within the diagram notation. The "(1,t)" indication of the number of times that the "Transaction" process is to occur tells us this. It says that the process is to be repeated until all transactions for that day have been processed, however many transactions that turns out to be. If necessary for documentation purposes, that physical test may be included on the Warnier-Orr diagram this way:

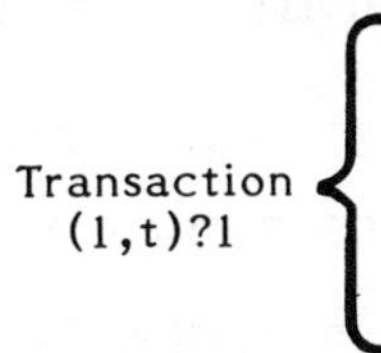


Figure 10.5: Physical Constraint

Then, we can include the actual expression of the physical test at the bottom of the test as a footnote:

NOTES:
?1 - end of transactions is true

This note allows us to include both the logical "number of times" designation (1,t) and the actual physical test which will be implemented in a program (end of transactions = true).

## Subroutines

Another reason that the test for the end of the day's transactions is not further defined is because of the varying ways that different computer programming languages handle repetitive calls of this type.

In the actual program code which will be written, the process "Transaction" will become what is called a subroutine. That name is indicative of the function that subroutines play in the computer program--they are routines which are performed within other larger routines. In this case, the "Transaction" process will be a subroutine to the process "Day." Similarly, the "Day" process is a subroutine within the "Month" process, and so on.

The way in which various computer programming languages handle subroutine invocations is not at all consistent. Some languages, like COBOL and PL/1, will allow the subroutine invocation itself to make the test for the end of the repetition. These type of subroutine calls generally are worded something like this:

```
DO TRANSACTION-PROCESS UNTIL END-OF-TRANSACTIONS IS TRUE.
```

Figure 10.6: Subroutine Invocation Type 1

so that no actual test of the condition "End of Transactions" is ever specifically written in the "End Transaction" process.

Other languages, which include some versions of BASIC, RPG, Assembler, and FORTRAN, do not have such a test which can be tied to the subroutine invocation. In these cases, a specific test within the program is required, and these tests are of the form:

```
LABEL:   EXECUTE TRANSACTION-PROCESS
         IF END-OF-TRANSACTIONS IS FALSE
          THEN GO BACK TO THE INSTRUCTION AT "LABEL".
```

Figure 10.7: Subroutine Invocation Type 2

Since we are striving for a design which is, as much as we can make it, language independent, then incorporating further any specific test for the end of a repetitive process into our design would be a mistake. This is a relatively trivial task which may be standardized for any particular language. Therefore, we leave the logical design alone.

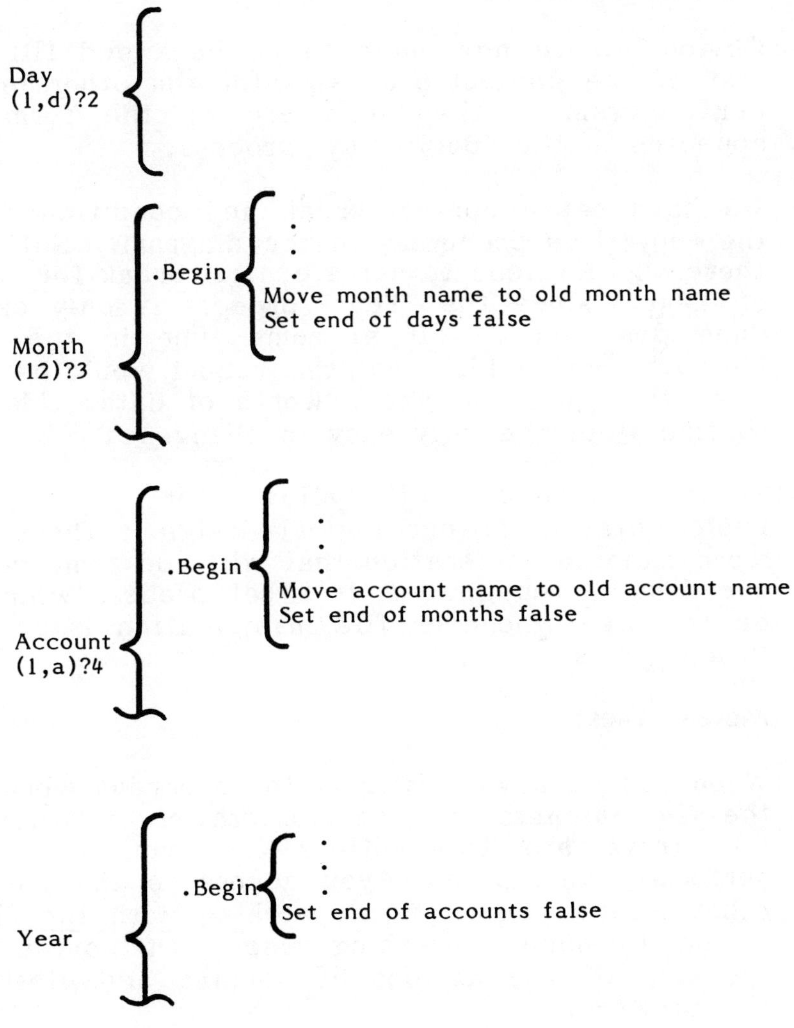


NOTES:
?2 - end of days = true
?3 - end of months = true
?4 - end of accounts = true

Figure 10.8: Additions to Logical Design

## More Control Breaks

Obviously, we now have to go back and fill in the rest of the control processes for the other levels of our diagram. They also are of the form which appeared in the "Begin Day" process.

We have set a control break and conditioned all of the repetitive processes in the diagram. Notice that there was no need to set a control break for the "End of Year," since the "Year" process is only executed once per report. If at some time in the future, however, we decided that this report would be run for more than just one year's worth of data, this yearly routine would be very easy to change.

These additions will allow for the physical implementation of our logical design. There is one more major consideration that will add some detail to our design, though. It is a set process which must be followed whenever file manipulation is performed in a process.

## More on Files

When you work with files in the everyday world, with the file cabinets and the file drawers familiar to us all, there are two actions that you must always perform. One permits you access to the files, the other allows you to finish working with the file and go on to doing something else. Of course, we're speaking of the actions of opening and closing the file drawers.

There is an analogous operation whenever computer files are accessed in a program. Before any records can be read from the file, it must be opened, and before the program can end, the file must be closed. These "openings" and "closings" cause the computer to perform a process which makes the data in the files available for us to use.

In most languages, the file opening and closing is done automatically by the computer whenever it runs across an instruction that says "OPEN TRANSACTION-FILE," or something very much like that. Usually we also need to tell the computer whether the file that is to be opened will be read from, written to, or both. This is accomplished by simply adding the word "input," the word "output," or the word "update" to the open statement, so that it looks something like "OPEN INPUT TRANSACTION-FILE," or "OPEN TRANSACTION FILE AS UPDATE."

These mandatory openings and closings occur for most processes in the "Begin Report" and the "End Report" routines. We'll simply need to tell the computer to open all of the files that we will use and then close all of them. This detail should be added to the logical design.

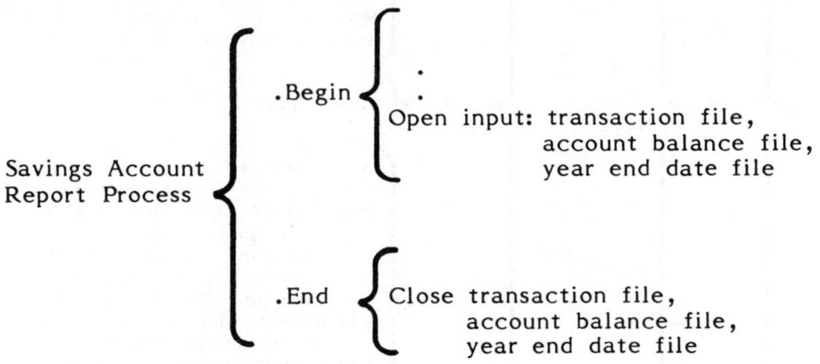


Figure 10.9: File Opening and Closing

Usually, although we need to tell the computer what type of file is to be opened, we don't have to specify the type when closing.

So now, this particular process design is complete, and is shown in it's entirety in Figure 10.10. This diagram is ready to be converted into a computer program. Since this process was not designed for a particular language on a specific computer, we are free to choose the language (and sometimes even the computer) that it will be programmed in. And this diagram, along with the rest of the diagrams generated in order to produce it, offer a complete

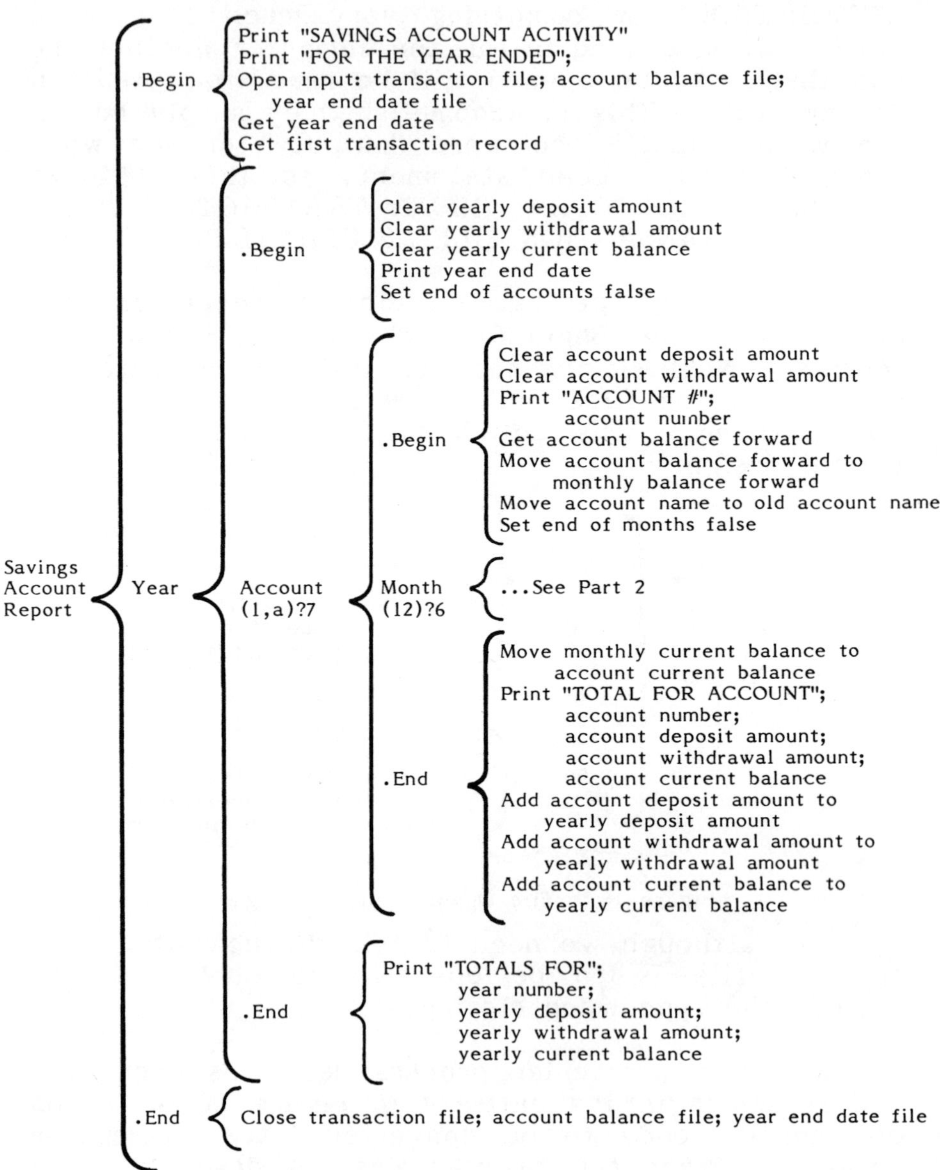


Figure 10.10: Completed Savings Account Report - Part 1

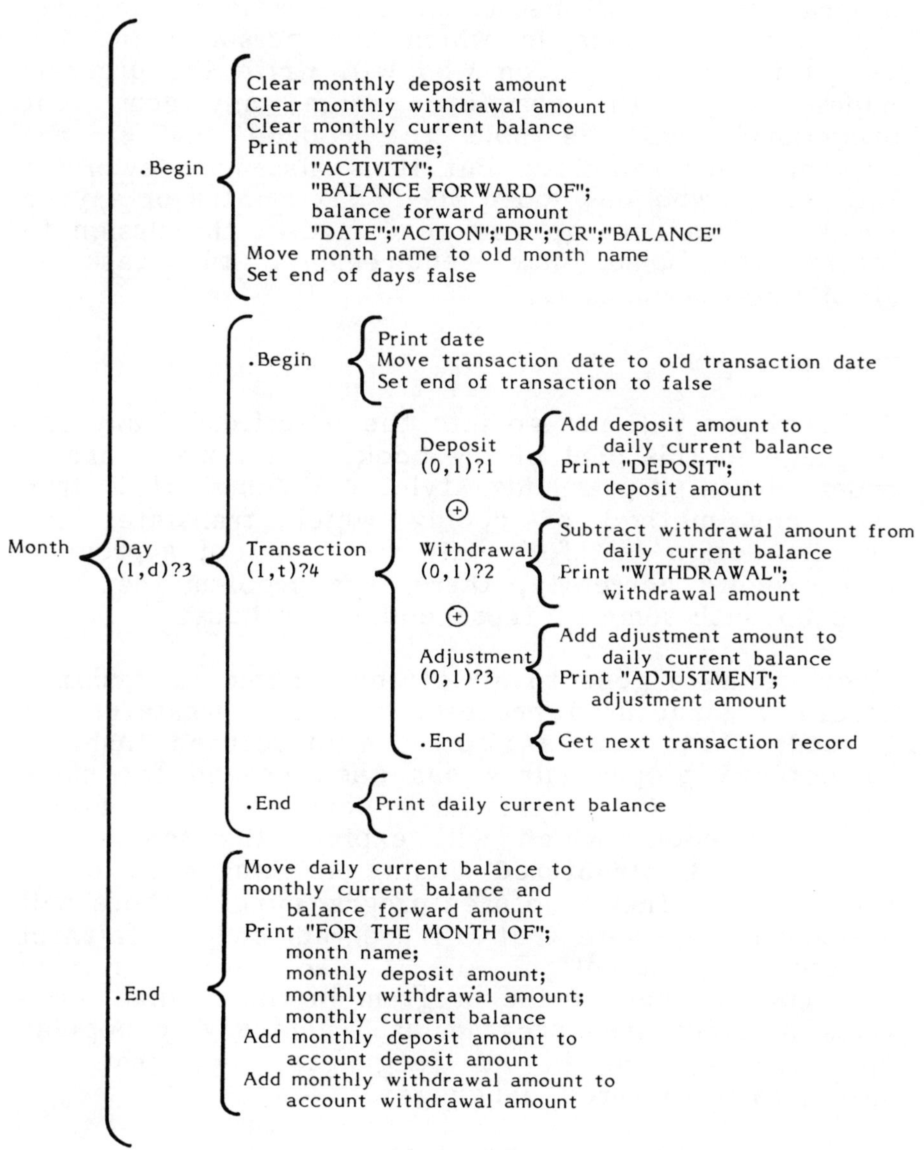


Figure 10.10: Completed Savings Account Report - Part 2

and understandable documentation package for the program which will be written. This is particularly nice for the cases in which the person doing the design is not the person who will write the program code. Given the complete design, any competent programmer will be able to produce the correct program very rapidly. But it is also nice even for the person who developed it--in six months or a year when you want to go back and modify the design to incorporate some new requirement, the task is simplified enormously.

## Programming

Although we will not go into the specifics of any one language in this part of the book, a few words are in order about programming style. Although it is true that any method of coding which translates the process design faithfully into some sort of a program will execute correctly, there is a problem that may crop up with some of those coding methods.

Since we have gone to all of the trouble to design a carefully structured process, it seems wasteful not to code that process also in a structured fashion. "Structured programming" has been around for many years now, and there are dozens of excellent reference books which will explain the tenets and the rules of structured coding in languages other than BASIC. The structured programming methods will allow you to ensure that the program code is faithful to the program design, and it also allows for very easy maintenance of the program in the future. The rules of structured program are, contrary to popular opinion, valuable in all languages, not just the so-called "structured" languages.

## EXERCISES

1. Complete the physical portion of the design for the problem at the end of Chapter 9.

# 11

# Common Mistakes and Questions

## Common Errors

Newcomers to this Warnier-Orr program design methodology often have many questions about their work. They want to know whether or not what they are doing is correct; whether the diagrams they have done are complete; etc. In order to be of some use to the potential programmer, this chapter attempts to anticipate and answer some of the more common questions that are usually asked, as well as trying to forewarn the program designer of some technical mistakes that are commonly made.

## Philosophical Errors

Many first-time users of the Warnier-Orr diagrams tend to make mistakes in their use that occur in so many cases that they are worth examining. The biggest and most common mistakes tend to be in an area that we can call "philosophical" errors. These errors are not really a misuse of the techniques so much as a misunderstanding of the techniques. By far the most common error stems from the fact the computer programmers tend to be obsessed with the desire to write some kind of code at the very beginning of the design process.

People who are just beginning to learn a programming language do not have this problem at first. However, those people who are already familiar with a programming language sometimes get into real difficulties because of this tendency.

The problem usually manifests itself with any or all of the following three practices:

1. Trying to code the program while designing it (called the "design-a-little, code-a-little approach)
2. Relying too heavily language restrictions and considerations while doing to logical design
3. Skipping the design phase altogether because:
   a) The program is "too easy", or
   b) The programmer is "too smart"

Any of the above practices will, at worst, destroy most if not all of the effectiveness of the Warnier-Orr methodology, and at best will certainly cause you to waste a great deal of time.

## Design-a-little, Code-a-little

Trying to build a logical design using the first technique--the "design-a-little, code-a-little" approach, will probably cause you to waste a considerable amount of time. This technique of designing and programming at essentially the same time will also require that you waste a great deal of valuable effort, for which your returns are few and far between.

Invariably, while designing/coding in this manner, you will run across a coding problem that will necessitate a change in the portion of the design already completed. At this point, you will also have to go back and rework the part of the code that corresponds to this part of the design. This is called "coding yourself into a corner," and, like the old problem of painting yourself into a corner, it can only be corrected by making a mess of the rest of the job.

Also, when you finally do get around to completing a program with this method, it tends to be about twice as long and about half as efficient as it should have been if you had done the design first and then the program. And, you will probably be in for quite a lot of what are called debugging runs. A debugging run is an attempt to correct the program by running it on the computer to see if it works. If it doesn't, you have to find out what is wrong, and then try to fix it and run it again. Invariably, the "design-a-little, code-a-little" practice produces more that its share of incorrectly spelled instructions, inconsistent data field names and missing data elements. All in all, it seems that this method of writing programs leaves a lot to be desired.

## Reliance on Coding Statements

The second technique described above is a common mistake that veteran programmers almost always seem to make: that of relying too heavily on the program language they will be using while doing the program design. Consider the two examples of program "designs" illustrated in Fugure 11.1 and 11.2.

The same process is shown in both of the above diagrams--it is a fairly standard method for the computation of overtime wages. The diagram of Figure 11.1, however, seems to be the type of diagram that veteran programmers will almost always try to draw. The programmer that produced this diagram has relied heavily on the actual instructions of a language like BASIC or FORTRAN. For those of us not familiar with either of those languages, this kind of a diagram is essentially unreadable. It looks like so much gibberish.

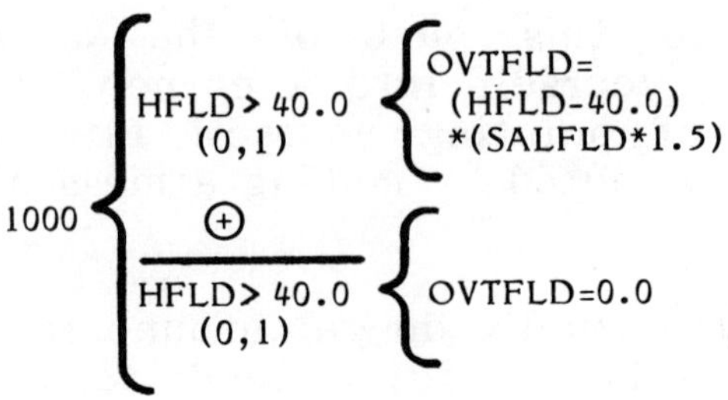


Figure 11.1: Design #1

Compute Overtime Pay

Hours Worked>40
(0,1)

Set overtime pay =
(hours worked over 40) times
(salary at time and one-half)

⊕

Hours Worked>40
(0,1)

Set overtime pay = zero

Figure 11.2: Design #2

Contrast that way of diagramming with that shown in Figure 11.2. This diagram correctly details the logical process for the computation of overtime wages. It is very clear and very readable.

You can see that if a design looked something like Figure 11.1, anyone besides the person who created it would have a hard time understanding it, even if they were familiar with FORTRAN or BASIC. Anyone who did not know either of those languages would not be able to tell at all what this part of the design was supposed to be doing. Ultimately, with hobby computers, it isn't that we are particularly concerned with other people being able to read part of someone's work, it is that in six months or a year even the person who created the diagram won't be able to read or understand it. This means that instead of being able to build on work already completed, we must go back and start over again. Reinventing the wheel wastes a lot of resources.

On the other hand, it is impossible to misunderstand what the process diagrammed in Figure 11.2 is doing. It is very easy to read and comprehend because it shows the logical side of the procedure. Even people who didn't know the first thing about computers could pick up this diagram and would be able to understand it.

This stress of the logical over the physical while designing with the Warnier-Orr diagrams is essential to their correct usage. Designing as in Figure 11.1 serves absolutely no purpose as far as understanding the process that is being described, and on top of this, such diagrams are absolutely worthless as far as documentation is concerned.

As long as we're on the subject, it might be worthwhile to mention that through the development period of this technique, some people were concerned that the heavy stress on the logical side of the problem with the diagrams might render them essentially worthless as documentation aids. The worry was that because of the reliance on the logical problem rather than the physical, the diagrams might become so far removed from the "real world" as to render them ineffective and inaccurate. Those fears were easily put aside with two simple diagramming and coding conventions.

1. Physical mileposts on the Warnier-Orr diagrams
2. Logical symbol tables in the programs

Thus, when we actually wrote code for the diagram in Figure 11.2, we would tie it to the logical process by adding to the diagram:

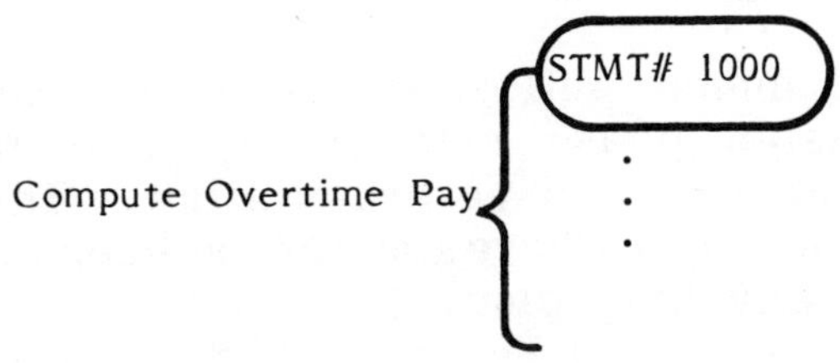


and we would include in the program itself some comments which linked that portion of code to the diagram that it came from:

```
          .
          .
          .
1000 ***       COMPUTE OVERTIME PAY
1001 ***          HFLD    = WOURS WORKED
1002 ***          OVTFLD  = OVERTIME PAY
1003 ***          SALFLD  = SALARY
          .
          .
          .
```

The asterisks on the lines of pseudo-code above indicate that these lines are comments inserted into our program, and not actually executable instructions. For BASIC programs these would take the form of REMinder statements.

This convention allows us to have a very clear and concise, one-to-one mapping between the logical diagram and the physical code, and reference between them becomes quite easy. If, for instance, you want to know what a particular section of code is supposed to be doing, you need only to look it up on the logical diagram. Similarly, if you want to find out which part of the program is carrying out a particular logical function, you have the information at your fingertips as to where to look. This is excellent documentation in the event that you or someone else might someday want to make a modification to your code.

## Skipping the Design Phase

The third common philosophical error, that of skipping the design phase altogether, is a real problem to both newcomers and veterans alike. The reason for it lies more in the realm of subconscious human nature than anything else.

If you look at a productivity curve for a programmer who is introduced to the Warnier-Orr diagrams, it generally looks something like the curve in Figure 11.3.

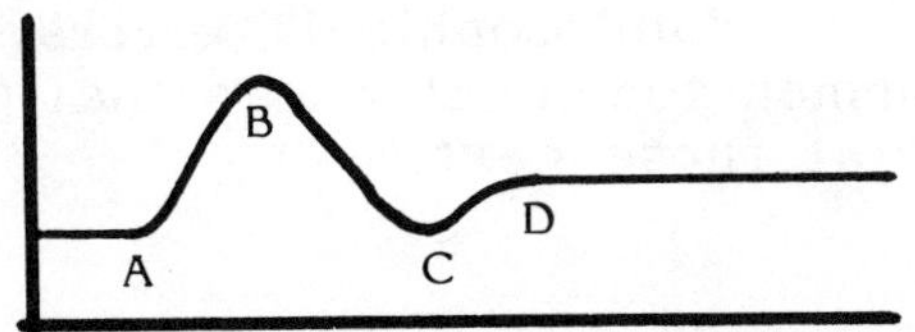


Figure 11.3: Programmer Productivity

A currently productive programmer will be producing work at a constant rate up until the time he is introduced to the Warnier-Orr techniques (at point A). He will typically show an initial burst of very high productivity (point B) which occurs as a result of having been given a better tool with which to do programming work. This is usually shortly followed by a slump (point C) where the programmer sinks back to or just above his previous level of work. Eventually, he will climb back up to a new, higher level of work (point D), where he will usually stay.

This peculiar slump at point C seems to be primarily due to the fact that since the programmer has begun to feel comfortable with the new technique and has had some initial success with it, he begins to feel confident enough to try to do the same quality of work without doing the diagrams first. So he begins to omit the design phase of programming and tries to do the same work with just the code. He soon realizes that the quality of his work has dropped off, and that he isn't getting the same good results that he was getting before and starts to do the diagrams once again, this time for good. His productivity rises up to a new, higher level that will remain fairly constant from then on.

Apparently, the only way to get new people to avoid this temptation is to forewarn them that it does tend to happen, so that if and when they find themselves on the downhill side of the productivity curve, they can recognize the trap in time to escape the worst of it.

So much for the "philosophical" errors. There are also a few common technical errors that people make, and we'll look at those next.

## Technical Errors

For a lot of people who are just starting to program and may be unfamiliar with "structured" programming techniques, some of the diagramming methods may seem to be a bit uncomfortable. One of the most frequently seen of the "technical" errors is the attempted use of a "GO TO" statement on the diagram. For example, consider the CASE statement illustrated in Figure 11.4.

```
                 { Product Code = A { unit price is in
                 {    (0,1)         {  price field #1
                 {                  {
                 {                  { Go To End Price
                 {       ⊕
                 {                  { unit price = $7.00
                 { Product Code = B {
Determine Unit   {    (0,1)         { Go To End Price
    Price        {
                 {       ⊕
                 { Product Code = C { Go To Compute Market
                 {    (0,1)         {    Price
                 {
                 {  End Price
```

Figure 11.4: Attempted Use of "GO TO's"

Two of the occurrences of the GO TO's in Figure 11.4 are incorrect and the other is ambiguous. The GO TO's in "PRODUCT CODE = A" and in "PRODUCT CODE = B" are unnecessary and incorrect. The default logical linkages will see to it that the appropriate steps are executed. The GO TO at "PRODUCT CODE = C" is unclear; if it is supposed to mean that we are to cease execution of this process and jump to the procedure "COMPUTE MARKET PRICE" to begin processing, then its usage is incorrect. If on the other hand it means that

"COMPUTE MARKET PRICE" is a common utility routine and is described elsewhere in the system, then the GO TO is misleading. We should have instead written the alternative, as shown in Figure 11.5.

Product Code = C (0,1) { Compute Market Price ...SEE PAGE #3

Figure 11.5: Offpage Reference

if the process was expanded on a different page of the diagram, or something like the words "...SEE ABOVE" or "...SEE BELOW" if that process appears elsewhere on the same page. Besides that, the GO TO is a physical entity to be used at execution and is not a logical process. Hence, it does not belong on a logical Warnier-Orr diagram.

Another common technical mistake is one that is a little harder to catch. Consider the CASE statement in Figure 11.6.

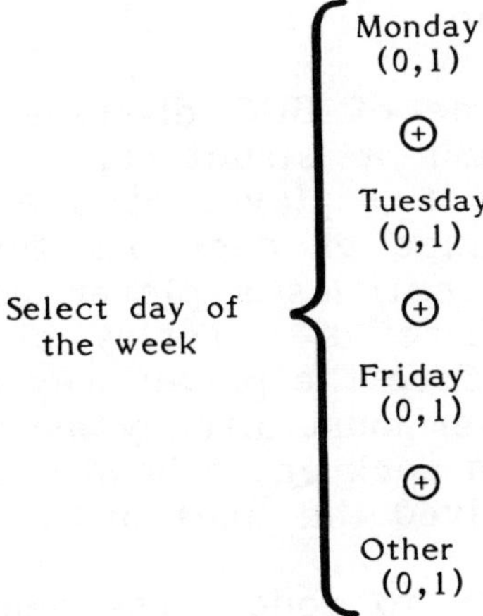


Figure 11.6: A CASE Statement

Note that in this CASE statement, not only are the processes outlined mutually exculsive (only one of the cases can be true), but they are also mutually independent (that is, their order within the CASE statement does not matter). It would be just as correct for someone to have written

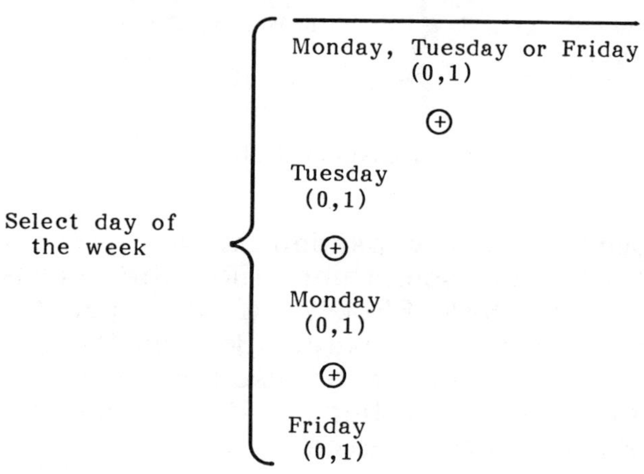


Figure 11.7: Equivalant CASE

However, in some instances you will run across a structure that looks like it should be a CASE statement, but it is not.

For instance, the game of BUG discussed in earlier chapters contains such a structure. During the playing of the game, if a player rolls a "4" on the die, there is a sequence of decisions that must be made. A roll of "4" entitles a player to receive a BUG antenna, but there is a series of conditions which must be met before the player may be awarded the antenna. The player must already have rolled for and received a body, a neck and a head and they must not have already received the limit of two antennae.

Many people would try to code those decisions as a CASE statement that looks like the one in Figure 11.8.

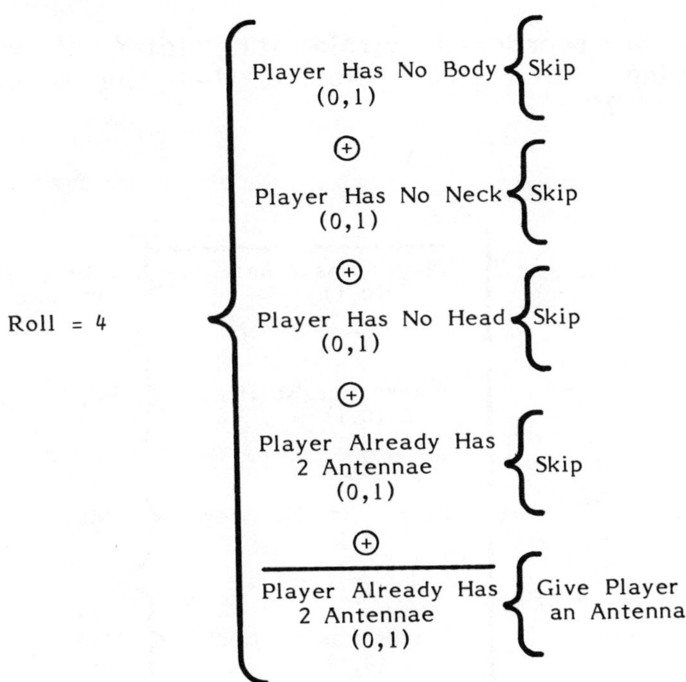


Figure 11.8: Presumed CASE Statement

The process in Figure 11.8 certainly looks correct, and indeed, if you write it as a CASE statement in structured narrative form, like Figure 11.9, it will even be performed correctly

```
If player has no body
    Then skip,
Otherwise If player has no neck
    Then skip,
Otherwise If player has no head
    Then skip,
Otherwise If player has two antennae
    Then skip,
Otherwise give the player one antenna.
```

Figure 11.9: Narrative of Conditions

But this process is not a CASE statement. It is more properly called a "pseudo-CASE" statement, because each of it's "cases" is mutually dependent; they cannot be reordered within the statement without destroying the logic. Notice that the scheme in Figure 11.10

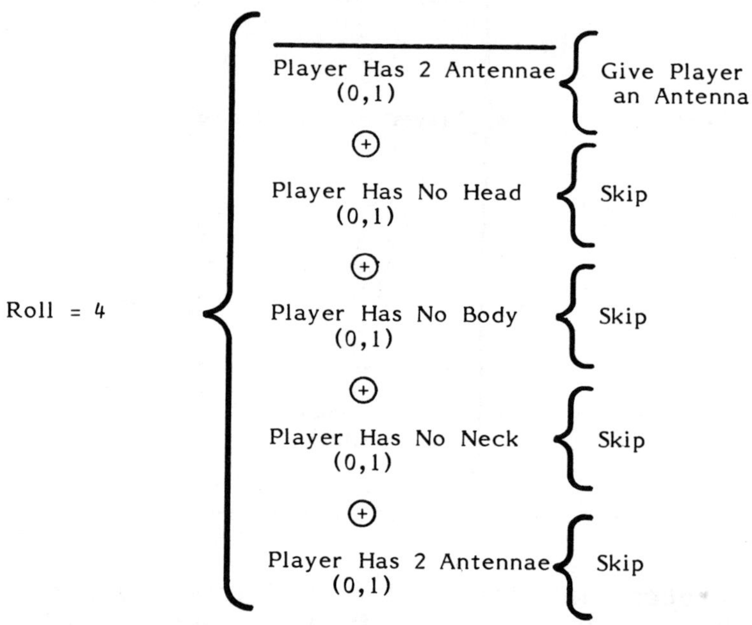


Figure 11.10: Incorrect Re-Ordering

does not work at all; it will give the player an antenna anytime he rolls a four, until he has two antennae, regardless of whether or not he already has a body, a neck, or a head. A more correct logical interpretation of that structure appears in Figure 11.11.

You might also notice that since the BUG must have a body before it can have a neck, and also must have a neck before it can have a head, if we merely check for the presence of the head, we will be indirectly checking for the neck and the body, so that the diagram shown in Figure 11.12 is an equivalant structure.

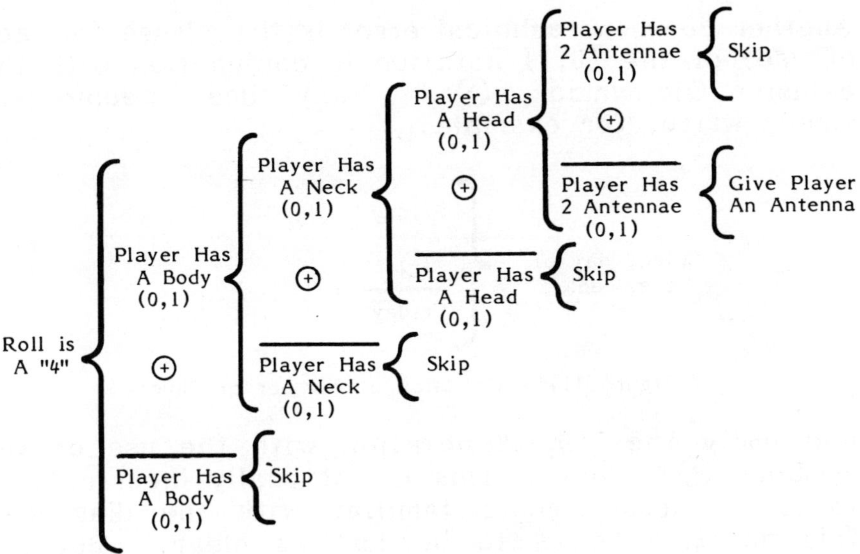


Figure 11.11: Correct Logical Structure

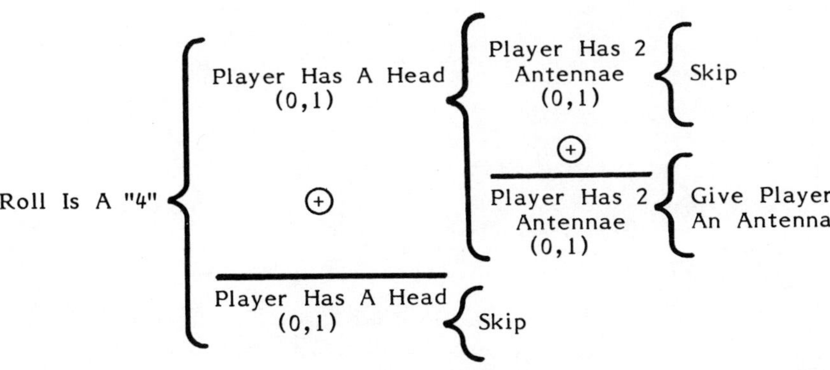


Figure 11.12: Another Interpretation

Another common technical error is the misuse (or lack of use) of the (0,1) notation in conjunction with the exlusive OR symbol "⊕." Many times, people will simply write, for example,

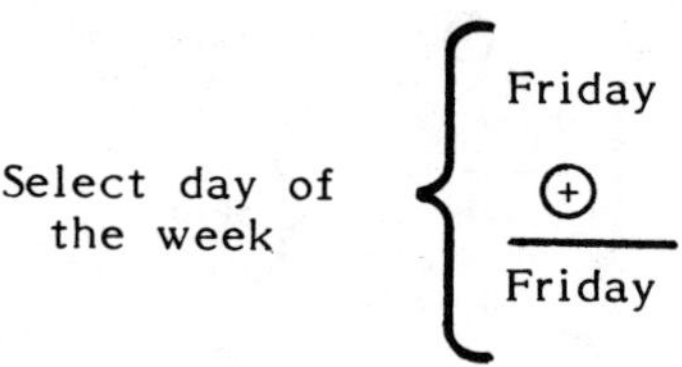


Figure 11.13: Omission of Number of Times

and imply the "(0,1)" notation with the use of the symbol "⊕" alone. This is not really incorrect, in fact, for most people familiar with the diagrams, this notation seems to be just as clear. But for users not quite so familiar with the Warnier-Orr diagrams it is probably best to go ahead and include the "(0,1)."

# 12

# Advanced Concepts:

## Concurrency

### Different Hierarchies

So far in this book, we have looked at only one type of hierarchical relationship: the type where the subset hierarchy fits neatly inside the set immediately above it. For instance, quarters fit neatly within years--there are four quarters in a year. Also months fit neatly within quarters, and days fit neatly within months. There are, however, some subdivisions of sets which do not fit neatly into our scheme of things. Look at the diagram in Figure 12.1, which is a type with which you should be familiar.

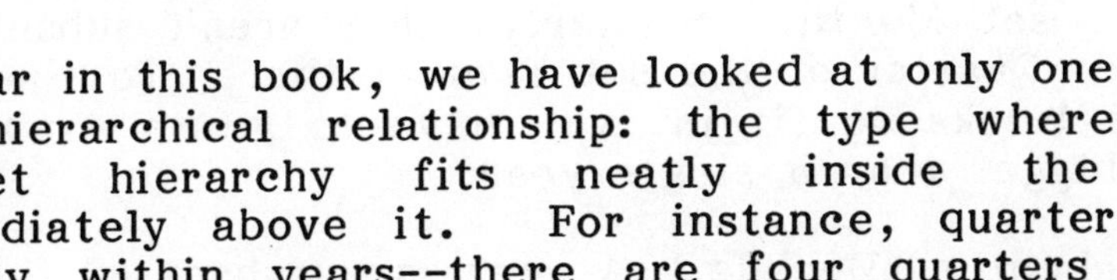

| Report Program | { | Years (1,y) | { | Quarters (4) | { | Months (3) | { | Days (1,d) | { |
|---|---|---|---|---|---|---|---|---|---|

Figure 12.1: Standard Temporal Hierarchy

This time hierarchy seems to describe all of the important subsets of the set "year." But there is one unit of time important in data processing that is often neglected in this kind of a hierarchical setup: and that is the set "week."

Where do weeks fit into the above diagram. Some people try to sandwich them in between "Months" and "Days," as in Figure 12.2.

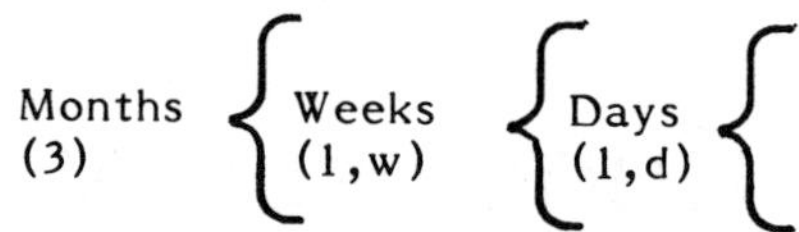


Figure 12.2: Attempted Solution

but this is not correct. The end of a Month only occasionally falls on a Friday or a Saturday (depending upon which day is to be considered the last day of the week). So Weeks aren't a subset of of the set Month. Similarly, they aren't subsets of the set Quarter or the set Year, either. To find out where Weeks do fit in, you have to go to a unit of time bigger than a single year.

How about a "Decade." A year is a subset of the set Decade, but the set Week is not. Neither is it a subset of the sets "Score" or "Century." To see the subset Week properly placed inside another time unit, you have to go up to a full cycle of the Gregorian Calendar, which is four hundred years. Every four hundred years,* a new cycle begins and a new weekly cycle is started. This cycle is represented on the Warnier-Orr diagram in Figure 12.3.

---

*

The Gregorian calendar is based on a 365 day year with a "leap" year of 366 days in every year which is evenly divisible by four, except those "century" years which are not evenly divisible by 400. So 1700, 1800, and 1900 were not leap years, but 2000 will be. The next cycle begins on Saturday, January 1, 2000.

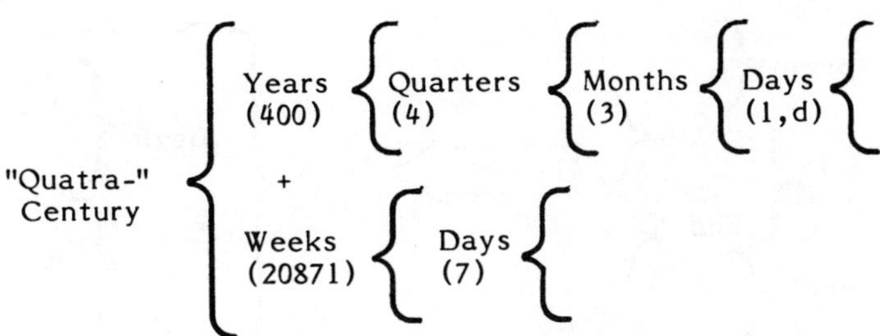


Figure 12.3: Proper Placement of the Subset "Weeks"

This notation, with the plus sign + between the two subsets, means that the two processes are operating side-by-side and at the same time. Thus, we call them concurrent operations. Concurrent operations are found occasionally in computer applications, and, although the relative number of these operations is quite small with respect to other types of operations (sequential and mutually exclusive), they invariably cause the most trouble because they are so hard to deal with. Up until around 1977, solving a concurrency problem involved quite a bit of thought and ingenuity.

Handling the problem of concurrency now is a relatively simple matter. Observe that both Year and Week both have a common subset: Days. Now, we can simply invert one of the concurrent hierarchies with respect to Days and map it back onto the other one. This isn't as hard or as complex as it sounds.

## Hierarchy Inversion

To invert a hierarchy, in this case Weeks with respect to Days, one drops the level of hierarchy to be inverted and moves the .Begin and .End processes for that level down to the very beginning and the very end of the level just below it, and conditions those processes to be performed (0,1) times. This process is illustrated in Figure 12.4

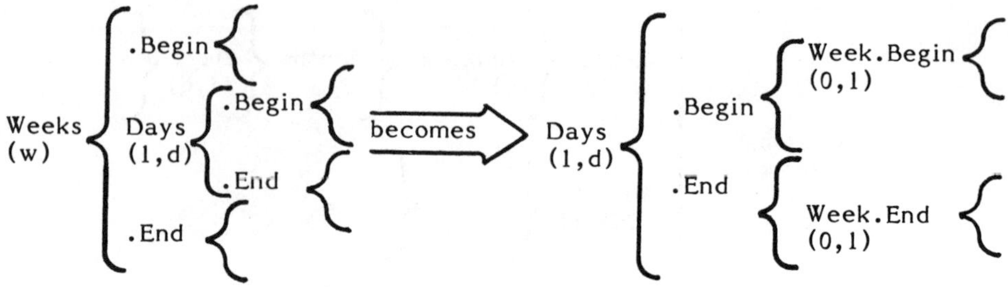

Weeks (w) { .Begin { ; Days (1,d) { .Begin { ; .End { } ; .End { }

becomes

Days (1,d) { .Begin { Week.Begin (0,1) { } ; .End { Week.End (0,1) { } }

Figure 12.4: Inverting a Hierarchy

The Week.Begin will be done (whenever it occurs) at the beginning of the day before anything else, so it appears within the Day.Begin process. Similarly, the Week.End process will be done only after all of the other daily processing is finished, hence it becomes the last process in the Day.End bracket.

The inverted diagram works this way: for each day that we process, we first check to see if this day is the beginning of a week. If it is, we then perform the Week.Begin process. Otherwise we go on to our normal daily processing. At the end of each days work, we check to see if this day is the end of a week, and if it is, we perform the Week.End procedure. In this way, we could even process five-day business weeks which begin on Monday and end on Friday.

Functionally, the normal hierarchy and the inverted hierarchy are equivalent--in operation they will both produce the same results. The inverted hierarchy, however, needs an extra test each day to properly interpret the inverted level, whereas the normal hierarchy does not require such a test.

There is no limit to the number of hierarchies that we can invert. If we had wanted to, we could have inverted the Yearly hierarchy with respect to Day. The result of this inversion is shown in Figure 12.5.

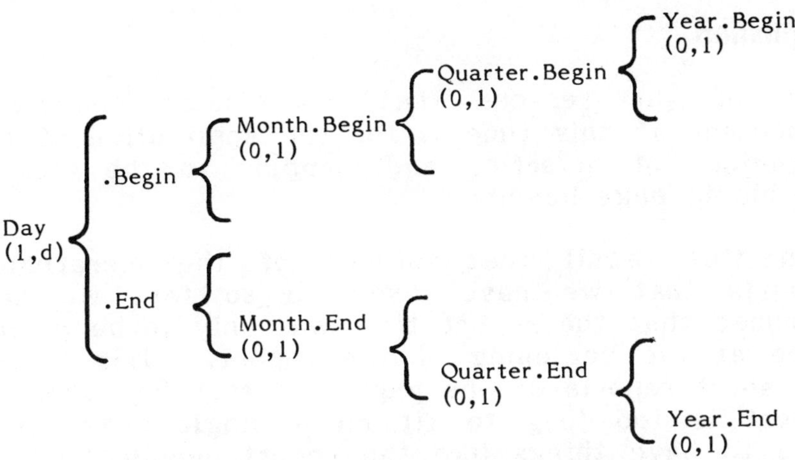


Figure 12.5: Inverted Yearly Hierarchy

## Mapping

The second step to handling our concurrent processes is to then map the inverted hierarchy back onto our desired diagram. In this case, we simply add the Week.Begin and the Week.End processes to the Daily routine.

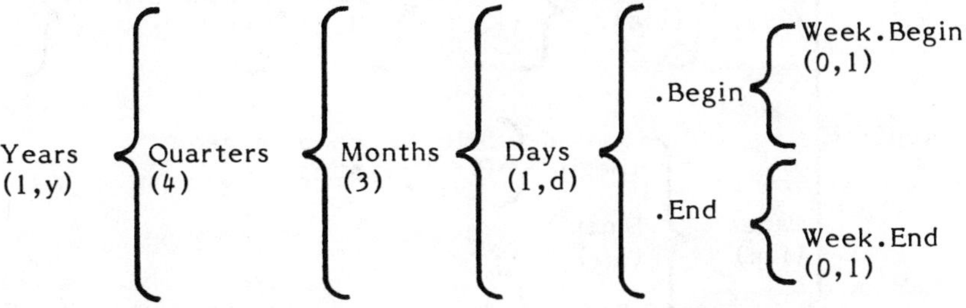


Figure 12.6: Mapping the Inverted Hierarchy

This gives us a diagram which is functionally equivalent to the one pictured in Figure 12.3, but has no concurrencies. Now, if we have any actions which need to be done Weekly, we have a place to put them where they will be properly taken care of.

## Pagination

One of the reasons that we discuss concurrent processes at this time is for the application of this technique of inverting and mapping to the task of producing page headings.

You will recall that on all of the hierarchical reports that we have discussed so far, we have assumed that the report title was only to be printed once at the beginning of the report. This is fine for short reports of one page or less. But when the report is too long to fit on a single page, it is nice to have things like the report heading and the page number at the top of each page of the report, or having the page heading at the top of the page and the page number at the bottom. So far, we have not discussed how this is done. This problem of printing the page number and the page heading at the beginning or end of each page of the report is solved by the reduction of two concurrent processes.

For our printed savings account report, the page heading situation is described by the following diagram:

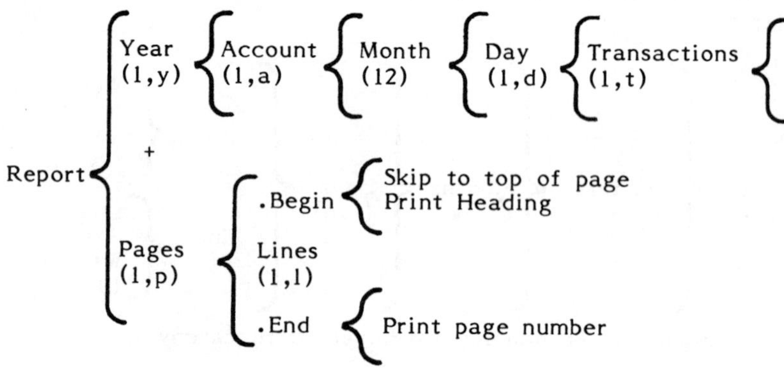


Figure 12.7: Concurrent Processes

Realizing that this representation of the page heading process is correct allows us to produce the solution quite easily. We invert the Page process with respect to Line and map it back onto our desired hierarchy at every place a line is to be printed.

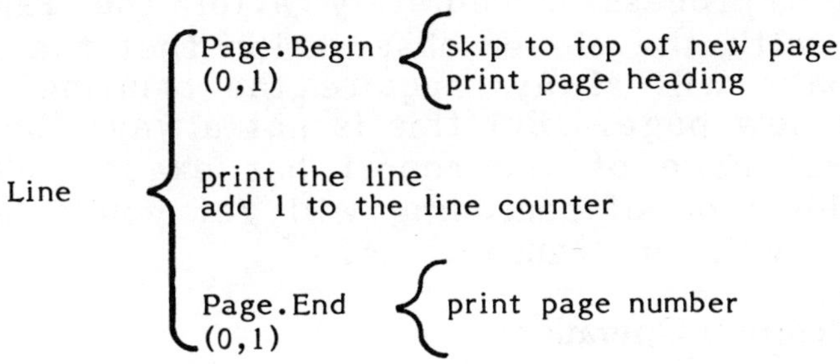


Figure 12.8: Solution to the Page Heading Problem

Then, all we need to do is set up a line counter so that our program will be able to tell when a page is full. Each time that we print a line, we'll add 1 to the line counter, thus keeping a running count of how many lines that have been printed on any particular page.

For a fixed page size of 50 lines per page, we'll add to our program the following logic:

Report.Begin { set page number = 0
set line counter = 51

Page.Begin { set line counter = 1
add 1 to page number

Figure 12.9: Line Counter and Page Number Manipulation

Then, the condition which triggers both the Page.Begin and Page.End processes is a test for whether or not the line counter is greater than (>) 50. By initially setting the line counter to 51, this causes the first page to be correctly printed.

You should verify that this process does indeed print a page heading and a page footing for each page, and that it does not do anything strange. Some veteran programmers have a problem when the number of transactions is an exact multiple of the number of lines per page: often they will try to put the Page.Begin process immediately after the Page.End process, with the clever observation that the end of an old page will always require the printing of the top of a new page. But this is not always the case. If the last page of the report has exactly 50 lines on it, this kind of reasoning will get you a heading on a page with no transactions.

## Other Concurrent Operations

There are other operations that crop up occasionally and should at least be acknowleged. We'll not go into any great detail in this section, as the proper treatment of this subject would fill another volume.

Most everyone who has worked around computers before is familiar with the concept of a computer terminal. Terminals are frequently found on large computers, and allow many people at many different sites to have access to the computer at the same time. These terminals consist of a keyboard or a card reader where information can be fed into the computer, and a CRT (cathode ray tube, or a television-type display screen for those not familiar with the terminology) or a printer to in turn receive information back from the computer.

All of these terminals are on at the same time, and they may all be running completly different programs, but they are all connected to a single computer.

How is this bit of wizardry accomplished? Well, the reason that we can do this is that the speed with which the computer can carry on arithmetic operations internally is an order of magnitude faster than the keyboards and printers can react. When just a single program is running on the computer, the internal part of the computer is actually just sitting there most of the time, waiting for information to be transferred in and out of the slow peripherals. A technique called multiprogramming allows us to use that dead time to go ahead and execute other programs. The actual methods that the computer uses to keep track of all of the different programs and to keep them separate from each other are far too complex to examine here except in the most general of terms.

If we were going to design such a multiprogramming system, we would want to design it hierarchically, like this:

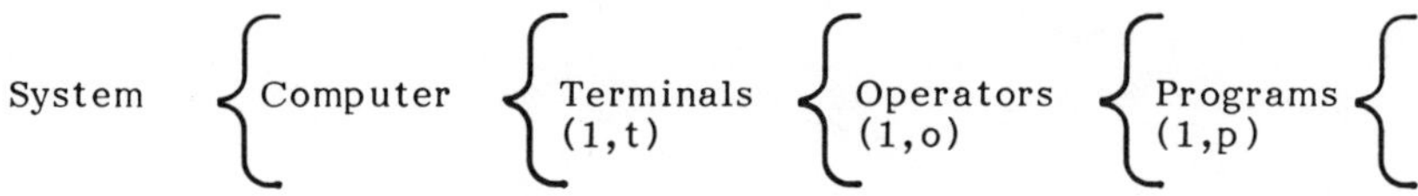


Figure 12.10: Multiprogramming Hierarchy

This looks just exactly like the type of diagram that we are already familiar with. And, if each terminal started and then quit in turn (with no two terminals operating at the same time) then this would be the appropriate diagram. But in our multiprocessing environment, that is not the case. Any or all of the terminals may be on and operating at the same time. This represents another type of concurrent operation, and we reflect it on the diagram like:

+Terminals {
(1,t)

Figure 12.11: Another Concurrent Operation

No terminal may have more than one person operating it at the same time, and no operator can have more than one program executing at the same time, so that our diagram is now correct.

# 13

# Advanced Concepts: Assembly Line Diagrams

## Systems Considerations

Through this portion of this book, we have examined the techniques for creating what has been called a program design. That is, how one manipulates an output to design and eventually construct a single program.

But in a general sense, this is an unrealistic viewpoint of the world. Very few outputs, when actually decomposed and examined, will result in the design of just one single program. More often than not, the examination of this output will result in a whole family of programs, or the output will turn out to be just one of many related outputs that collectively form what is called a system.

A system is defined to be a set of actions which perform an integrated and total response to a problem. In lots of cases, a system could consist of only one program. Most computer games are complete systems, due to the fact that they do not depend on the working of any other program in order to succeed.

However, outputs such as hierarchical reports usually require more than just one program in order to run successfully. Or, when computers with a limited amount of memory space are used, large program often have to be broken up into several smaller pieces which individually will fit into the machine. This is also looked upon as a system.

One tool that is helpful in doing an entire systems design is an offshoot of the Warnier-Orr diagram called the assembly line diagram.

## Assembly Lines

The reason this type of a diagram is called an assembly line diagram will become quite apparent as we examine it. The philosophy of the diagram is the same as that behind the rest of the methodology: start with the output and work backwards. For a non-computer example, let us look at how one would develop an assembly line diagram for the process of building a car.

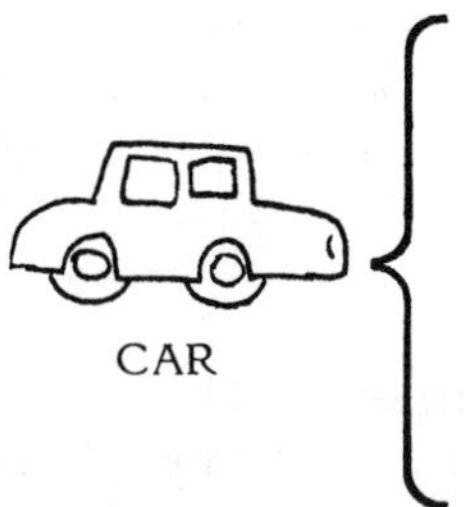


Figure 13.1: A Finished Car

To begin with, we start with the output: a finished car. Then we can break the process of building the car down one step by asking the question, "What can we most easily remove from this car?"

Probably the easiest thing to remove from the car is the hubcaps. So, if we were given everything else on the car already put together and ready to go, four hubcaps, and someone with a rubber mallet to hammer them onto the car, then producing a car from this point would be relatively trivial.

Figure 13.2: The Last Step to Assemble a Car

Each of these three components come together to form the finished product--a completed car. They are shown in the diagram of Figure 13.2 in concurrent fashion, as they are not sequential steps to be followed but rather are three elements which all come together at this point at the same time. The order in which we list them is not important, but all three must be present and combined before the next higher step is completed.

Our next step is to take the car without the hubcaps and take one more thing off of it. Probably the tires would come off next. So, given a car now without any tires, four tires, some lug nuts, and someone with a wrench to put them on the car, we could produce the car without any hubcaps.

In this way, we continue to disassemble all of the major components of the final product, so that whenever we stop at the far right-hand side, the elements that are left become the necessary inputs to the system--the vats of rubber, the sheets of steel, the paint, etc. The assembly line diagram then shows how those inputs come together to form our desired result.

In this same way, we can decompose a computer process to find out all of the functional pieces that is is made up of. The analysis of these functional steps will pinpoint all of the different processes which must be executed to produce the results. We can then package these functional steps into as many programs as we need.

## Ideal Files

For the savings account report that we have been developing, we have already designed the Logical Data Base that we need to be able to correctly produce it; with the assembly line diagrams, we can now find out how to produce the Logical Data Base.

This process involves creating a series of ideal files. That is to say, for each step in the following decomposition, we are going to decide what is the ideal form of the information that we would like to be working with. Again, we start with the final output: the savings account report. If we were given the correct Logical Data Base for the report and the process for converting that LDB into the report (a report print routine), then we have already seen that we can produce this report. The LDB is made up of all the sorted transactions for the year.

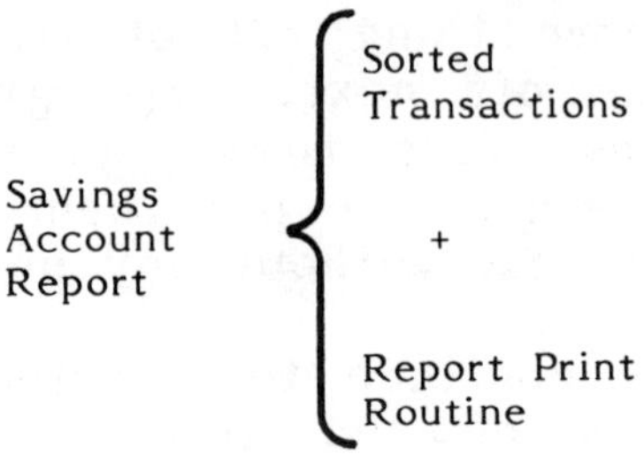


Figure 13.3: Savings Account Report Assembly

Since this file of sorted transactions is exactly what we need to be able to produce this report, we call it an ideal file.

The report print routine we already know how to develop. But how do we come up with the sorted transactions? If we had all of the transactions already gathered together in a single file, some capablity to sort that file (reorder the records in it), and the criteria for sorting the file (the desired order), then producing a sorted file would be very easy.

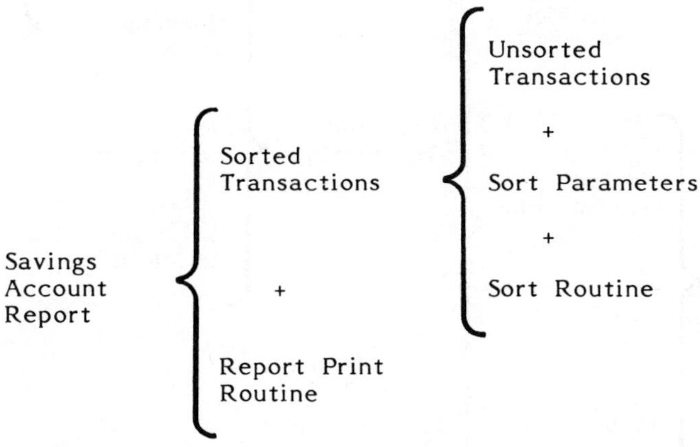


Figure 13.4: Producing Sorted Transactions

Next, we need to find out how to create an unsorted transaction file. The easiest way is to simply have someone enter those records into the computer one by one. However, we can't let them enter just anything into the computer--the data that is entered must be of a type which we can use in our program. We can't, for instance, allow someone to enter something like "$45t.00" for an amount, or a date like "2/30," etc. We must edit the incoming data for errors, and force the person entering the data to correct any mistakes that we can find.

When dealing with actions that must be performed by people for the machine, Murphy's law is the last word: anything that can go wrong will go wrong!

Therefore, we try to keep as many things from going wrong as we can, so that the answers we produce from the computer are as accurate and reliable as they can possibly be.

So on our next level of assembly line diagram, we reflect this needed data entry and data edit step. This added level of decomposition is shown in the diagram of Figure 13.5. At this point, we have come to an obviously human interface with the computer processing.

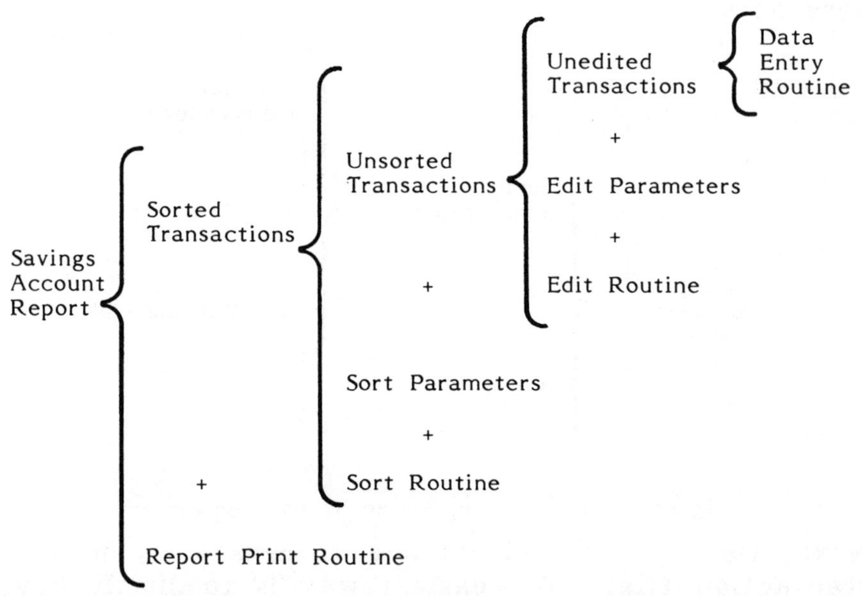


Figure 13.5: Data Entry/Edit Step

This diagram outlines the functional steps required to produce the savings account report. All of the elements which are to the far right of the diagram--i.e. all of the elements which do not expand into a subsequent bracket, become necessary inputs to the system.

Still to be decided however is the actual physical packaging of this savings account report process. That is, what parts of the assembly line break up into how many different programs? This is largely a function of the type of machine that you are going to be working with. If we have access to a large computer with a great deal of memory we could package this assembly line into one single program. If, however, we are working with a very small microcomputer with a very limited amount of memory, we could break the assembly line up into as many as five separate programs. When this is done, each one of the individual programs is referred to as a job step or a system step.

Probably for most computers, this particular problem would be broken up into two job steps--the report program already designed and a program which accepts, edits, and sorts the data into the report program's ideal file. Or, the program could be broken up into three job steps--the report program, a sort program, and an entry/edit program.

# 14

# Structured BASIC: Coding Conventions

## BASIC

The first portion of the book was intended to outline for the reader a general overview of the process for the development of a logical computer program design. Beginning with this chapter and continuing through the next, we will be taking a brief look at the process by which a program design developed in such a manner can be translated into a working computer program which has an excellent chance of running the first time. Since this book is directed primarily at the users of small business and/or hobby micro-computers, the language that will be used to present the examples will be the language BASIC.

BASIC is an acronym which stands for the Beginner's All-purpose Symbolic Instruction Code. It is just what it's name implies: a simple and basic computer language which is very easy to learn and very easy to use. BASIC is so easy, in fact, that many grade school children around the country are taught the language as their first exposure to the world of computer programming. But don't let this aspect of the language lower your opinion of it: in addition to being very easy to learn, BASIC, when used correctly, can be quite a powerful business and hobby programming language also.

Please note, however, that it is not the intention of the following two chapters to instruct the reader in the fundamentals of the BASIC language itself; rather, the following examples and techniques are presented to show how various aspects of the language can be applied within the logical design framework developed up to this point. It is assumed that the reader already has at least a passing familiarity with the format and the syntax of BASIC.

## Background

BASIC is a relatively old language, as computer languages go. It was originally developed back in 1963 and 1964 at Dartmouth College by Professors John Kemeny and Thomas Kurtz. Since that time the language has been changed and adapted so that it could be implemented on nearly every type of computer that has been developed. All versions of the language which conform to the standards of the original language are called "Dartmouth BASIC." Unfortunately, not many of the implementations of the language adhere to this standard: there are probably as many different versions of BASIC around as there are different types of computers which use the language. These versions vary so widely that it is quite rare to find any BASIC program written for one particular machine which will run on any other type of machine, without extensive modifications to the program (it has been facetiously suggested that any new vendor at a loss for a name for a new language developed for their computer will call the language BASIC).

Therefore, the BASIC which you will see used in the examples in the text probably will not look exactly like the version of the language which runs on your machine. This is not at all unusual and is not cause for alarm. It is quite easy to adapt the code developed here to run on most any computer. In fact, it is also advisable to adapt these conventions when working with other computer languages. The benefits gained will be approximately the same. But, in general, though, you will find that most of the instructions used in the following examples will not be far removed from whatever version of BASIC that you happen to be familiar with.

## Coding Conventions

Since so much time and effort has been spent up to this point in making certain that a program design is correct and logically structured, it seems to be worthwhile to take a little time to examine a consistent way that such a design could be implemented into program code. Neglecting such a step seems a lot like designing a bridge which is structurally correct, and then not being concerned with the type of materials which are actually used to construct it. While it is true to a certain extent that any method of coding which reproduces the logic of the design truly will be correct, problems which occur due to sloppy coding techniques show up with alarming regularity, and can undo much of the advantages gained by being careful in the design phase.

There are five program coding conventions which will be discussed in this chapter. And, although the comments made here apply specifically to BASIC, the rules and techniques suggested are just as valid for any other type of programming language which you happen to be using: FORTRAN, COBOL, Assembler, Pascal, APL, or even RPG II.

## Convention 1

Variable names should be indicative of variable function.

This convention ensures that any program code written will be as readable as it possibly can be.

Admittedly, this convention has little meaning in most implementations of BASIC--variable names are usually limited to a length of one or two characters, "X," "N1," "R$," etc., so that meaningful names are hard to come by.

However, some advantage is still gained by naming an amount field "A" or a total field "T" or "T1," if there is more than one total field in the program. For versions of the language which permit it, and certainly for other languages, variable names should be as close to the actual field name as possible. Some of the newer BASIC's being distributed today do allow variable names to be up to 32 and in some cases as many as 64 characters long. With such a capability, one can easily use names such as AMOUNT, MONTHLY-CREDIT-TOTAL, CUSTOMER-NAME, and so on.

Cute names or nonsense names such as SNEEZY, BILBO, HORSEFEATHERS, and HELL (a perennial favorite label with adolescent programmers, who can then literally tell their computer to GO TO HELL), should never be used. Such names serve absolutely no useful purpose in a program, and serve only to confuse and befuddle anyone else who tries to read the source code. Names like this will render an otherwise excellent program worthless.

Likewise, the extensive use of abbreviations and/or acronyms can detract from the readablilty of a program. CUSTOMER-MONTHLY-SALES is eminently preferable a name such as CSMNSLS.

### Convention 2

Comments should be used only when necessary.

This is particularly true in usually unreadable languages like BASIC. Comments can and should be used to explain complicated calculations and processes. They can also be used to augment the weakness of the BASIC's which do not allow for meaningful names. For instance, consider the passage from a BASIC program which appears in Figure 14.1.

```
120 REM OVERTIME CALCULATION ROUTINE
130 REM  O1 = OVERTIME AMOUNT
140 REM  H1 = EMPLOYEE HOURS WORKED
150 REM  W  = EMPLOYEE HOURLY WAGE
160 REM
170 REM OVERTIME-AMOUNT + EMPLOYEE-HOURS-WORKED
180 REM  OVER 40 TIMES EMPLOYEE-HOURLY-WAGE
190 REM  TIMES 1.5
200 O1=(H1-40.0)*(W*1.5)
```

Figure 14.1: Use of Comments

In languages that permit the longer variable names, comments of this type should be severly limited. A BASIC statement which looked like that of Figure 14.2 is perfectly readable and should not require any additional explanation. In such cases comments merely waste space. Also, comments are not likely to be maintained along with the actual executing statements in the code, and often will end up being incorrect or misleading after the code has been modified.

```
200 OVERTIME = (HOURS-WORKED - 40) * (WAGES * 1.5)
```

Figure 14.2: Using Meaningful Variable Names

**Convention 3**

Subroutines should be used to reflect program hierarchy.

Nearly all versions of BASIC allow for the use of subroutines. Some versions, however, severely limit the number of levels that subroutines can be nested (a subroutine called from within another subroutine is said to be nested). These versions are particularly difficult to work with, and should be avoided if at all possible. (Note: For the same reason, FORTRAN is difficult to use for structured coding. There is no allowance for the use of a local subroutine.) Allowances can be made for such languages, however variations which become too complex or cumbersome are often more trouble than they are worth. With the rapid proliferation of both hardware and software today, there is almost always an alternative BASIC available for any particular computer.

In utilizing this convention, each bracket of the logical program design will be translated into at least one subroutine (longer processes may require more than one subroutine--more about this in the following section). For instance, the diagram shown in Figure 14.3 would be coded as per the listing shown in Figure 14.4.

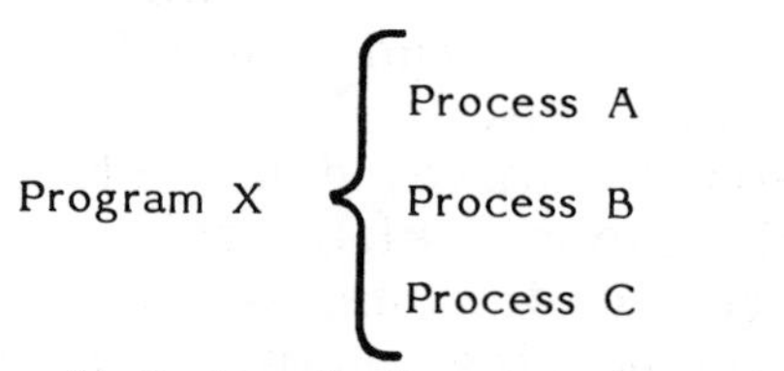

Figure 14.3: Sample Program Structure

When coded in this fashion, each section of the logical program design is reflected in one, small, specific module which can be easily understood. The use of this convention leads naturally into the next.

### Convention 4

Subroutines should be kept very small.

This further allows programs to be readable and clear. As a general rule of thumb, there should be no more than twenty lines of code in any one subroutine (excluding comment lines, when they are present). There are circumstances when the coding of a particular portion of a design will require more than twenty statements, but these instances will be relatively few. Most of the time, you will find that

```
PROGRAM X   10 REM PROGRAM X
            20 REM PROCESS A
            30 GOSUB 100
            40 REM PROCESS B
            50 GOSUB 200
            60 REM PROCESS C
            70 GOSUB 300
            80 END

PROCESS A   100 REM PROCESS A ROUTINE
              :
              :
            190 RETURN

PROCESS B   200 REM PROCESS B ROUTINE
              :
              :
            290 RETURN

PROCESS C   300 REM PROCESS C ROUTINE
              :
              :
            390 RETURN
```

Figure 14.4: Sample Coding Technique

subroutines will naturally be ten lines or less. When your subroutines become too large, they will become unreadable and unmaintainable. Large subroutines are sometimes also an indication of a flaw in the program design--a sign that perhaps still further decomposition of the problem is in order, so that some of the functions included in the large subroutine are broken down into separate, smaller subroutines.

**Convention 5**

GO TO's are to be avoided.

In languages like BASIC and Assembler, the nature of the language requires the use of GOTO's in certain instances. There are two valid uses of the GOTO in standard versions of BASIC. One allows the programmer to implement the repetative structure.

These structures, or "loops" are coded as in Figure 14.5 below.

```
100 REM PROGRAM.BEGIN
110 GOSUB 300
120 REM CUSTOMER (1,C)
130 GOSUB 400
140 IF E1=0 THEN GOTO 130
150 REM ...
```

Figure 14.5: Repetative Structure (DO-UNTIL)

The key to making this code work lies in the variable E1. This variable must be set to zero somewhere in the PROGRAM.BEGIN routine. Then, as you can see, the subroutine in line 130 will be called initially, and continue to be called over and over again until the value of E1 is changed to something other than zero. Thus, somewhere in the CUSTOMER routine, there must be a test for the "end of customers." When this test is true, E1 is set to some value other than zero. When that last occurence of the subroutine is completed and we again come to the test in line 140, the test in the IF statement is not true, and the program will continue on to execute lines 150 and below.

This is called the DO-UNTIL structure if you read the other literature in this area. It is used to implement loops which occur at least one time--(1,n) in our notation. For loops which occur (0,n) times, a different method of coding must be employed.

```
100 REM PROGRAM.BEGIN
110 GOSUB 300
120 REM CUSTOMER (0,C)
130 IF E1=0 THEN GOSUB 500 ELSE GOTO 150
140 GOTO 130
150 REM ...
```

Figure 14.6: Another Repetative Structure (DO-WHILE)

This type of loop is called the DO-WHILE, and, as you can see, requires two GOTO's to be implemented. This code allows for the case when there are no customers to process.

The other structure which sometimes requires the use of GOTO's is the alternative structure. Take as an example the following part of a diagram.

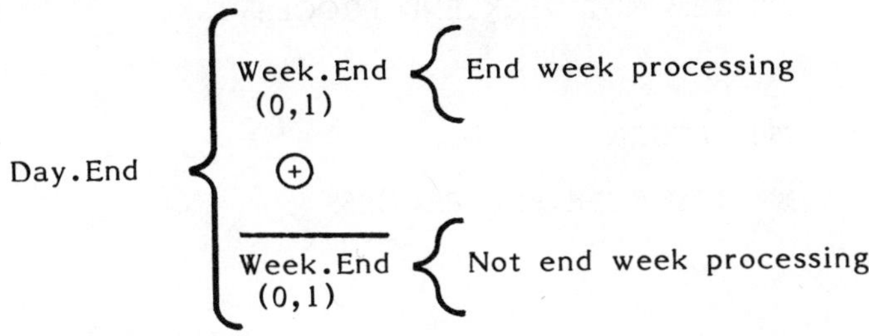


Figure 14.7: Simple Alternative Structure

This diagram could translate to a piece of code that looked something like this.

```
100 REM DAY.END
110 IF W1=0 THEN GOTO 200
120 REM WEEK.END PROCESS
     .
     .
     .
190 GOTO 300
200 REM NOT WEEK.END PROCESS
     .
     .
     .
300 RETURN
```

Figure 14.8: Alternative Code, Version 1

This method of coding must be used when the version of BASIC used does not permit the use of the ELSE clause of the IF statement. For versions of the language that do permit its use, then GOTO's are not necessary to implement this structure.

Notice that the physical test "W1=0" in both of the above cases translates to the logical condition "week end = false" (for consistency's sake a value of 0 in a test such as this will usually mean "false," while a value of 1 will mean "true"). One thing that many people like to do is set two variables "T" and "F" to

```
100 REM DAY.END
110 IF W1=0 THEN GOSUB 200 ELSE GOSUB 300
120 RETURN

200 REM NOT WEEK.END PROCESS
     .
     .
     .
290 RETURN

300 REM WEEK.END PROCESS
     .
     .
     .

390 RETURN
```

Figure 14.9: Alternative Code, Version 2

the value of 1 and 0 respectively at the beginning of their programs. Then, such tests will read W1=F or E1=T, and will be a little easier to understand.

For structures with more than two alternatives, the GOTO is often necessary, even for languages which permit the use of the ELSE clause in the IF statement. Take for example, the logic of the BUG program when determining the roll of the die. There are six alternatives. The preferable way to code this is as follows:

```
50 IF R=1 THEN GOSUB 100 ELSE IF R=2 THEN GOSUB 200
ELSE IF R=3 THEN GOSUB 300 ELSE IF R=4 THEN GOSUB 400
ELSE IF R=5 THEN GOSUB 500 ELSE IF R=6 THEN GOSUB 600
```

Figure 14.10: Roll of the Die CASE Statement

However, this line of code is usually far too long to be accepted by many versions of the language. If this is the case, then compensations have to be made which will allow us to mimic the same structure using a combination of a few shorter statements.

The code shown in Figure 14.11 will execute the same way that the single statement nested-IF would have, and can be used in most any version of BASIC.

```
10 IF R=1 THEN GOSUB 100 ELSE GOTO 20
15 GOTO 65
20 IF R=2 THEN GOSUB 200 ELSE GOTO 30
25 GOTO 65
30 IF R=3 THEN GOSUB 300 ELSE GOTO 40
35 GOTO 65
40 IF R=4 THEN GOSUB 400 ELSE GOTO 50
45 GOTO 65
50 IF R=5 THEN GOSUB 500 ELSE GOTO 60
55 GOTO 65
60 IF R=6 THEN GOSUB 600
65 REM END CASE
```

Figure 14.11: Another CASE Statement

One other point deserves mention here. Look closely at the code of Figure 14.11. The GOTO's on the odd-numbered lines may seem to be extraneous and not useful to some people. After all, the following piece of code, without the GOTO's, will also work.

```
10 IF R=1 THEN GOSUB 100
20 IF R=2 THEN GOSUB 200
30 IF R=3 THEN GOSUB 300
40 IF R=4 THEN GOSUB 400
50 IF R=5 THEN GOSUB 500
60 IF R=6 THEN GOSUB 600
70 . . .
```

Figure 14.12: CASE Statement?

This method of coding a CASE statement is correct in this instance, but it is sometimes misleading to use because it does not always work. Imagine what would happen to the logic if for some reason the value R needed to be changed in one of the called

```
10 IF X=1 THEN LET X=10
20 IF X=2 THEN LET X=9
30 IF X=3 THEN LET X=8
40 IF X=4 THEN LET X=7
50 IF X=5 THEN LET X=6
60 IF X=6 THEN LET X=5
70 IF X=7 THEN LET X=4
80 IF X=8 THEN LET X=3
90 IF X=9 THEN LET X=2
100 IF X=10 THEN LET X=1
```

Figure 14.13: Wrong CASE Implementation

subroutines. When such an event happens, all bets are off, because that method of coding falls apart. Try to decipher what happens in the code shown in Figure 14.13.

The purpose of this CASE statement seems obvious to anyone who looks at it: it is meant to give the 10's complement to the number at X. But does it work? Run a few trial values of X through this code and see what you come up with. Somehow, you can never get a number to come out to be 6 or more, no matter what number goes in! This is the reason that the ELSE clause and the GOTO are needed to make such a structure work. You will notice that had we implemented this code in the same way that we implemented the original CASE statement, it would indeed do what it was intended to.

# 15

# Structured BASIC: Structured Coding

## Coding

In this chapter, we will develop the code for the two major examples that we have traced throughout this book: the savings account program, and the BUG program. We will go into the specifics of the BUG program first, since it tends to be a little simpler and is probably a better introduction to some of the more fundamental concepts. The savings account report program will also be developed, although not in quite as much detail.

## The BUG Program

In order to be ready to code the logical design which we have created, we need to have at least three of the documents that we came up with during the development process close at hand and ready to refer to. We will need to have (1) a sample of the output that we originally wanted, (2) the logical data structure of the output, and (3) the logical process diagram for producing the output. With these in hand, we are ready to begin the coding process.

To begin with, we need to code the "root" portion of the program, i.e., the highest level of the process diagram. In order to do this for the Bug program, we are going to be referring to the diagrams of Figure 9.22 and 9.23 back in Chapter 9. In Figure 9.23, you will notice that the highest level of the process is divided up into three sections: the Program.Begin, the Game, and the Program.End. These we will code according to the conventions outlined in the last chapter. Remember, each level of hierarchy is going to be represented by a subroutine call, in BASIC this is the GOSUB statement.

```
10 GOSUB nnn
20 GOSUB nnn
30 IF E1=0 THEN 20
40 GOSUB nnn
50 END
```

Figure 15.1: Program Root

The code listed in Figure 15.1 represents all of the necessary instructions to correctly execute the first level of the BUG program as it was designed. However, this portion of the code, as written, is not very readable. Although it is correct and logically constructed according to the conventions, it is not as good as it could be. To make this code a little bit easier to follow, we will add a few well placed comment lines. That will enable us to locate this section of code in our logical design. Thus, we can reference either the design from a section of the code or vice versa, if and when the need arises.

```
 7 REM ************************
 8 REM BUG PROGRAM
 9 REM  PROGRAM.BEGIN
10 GOSUB aaa
19 REM  GAME (1,G)
20 GOSUB bbb
30 IF E1=0 THEN 20
39 REM  PROGRAM.END
40 GOSUB ccc
50 END
```

Figure 15.2: Using Comments in Code

Since we are coding this program from the top to the bottom, we are not yet sure of the exact statement numbers for the called subroutines. Therefore these statement numbers, indicated now by "aaa," "bbb," and "ccc," will be filled in as those parts of the code develop.

Notice how the code for the highest level will execute:

1. First, the routine for the beginning of the program is executed (GOSUB aaa).

2. When the Program.Begin process is finished, the GAME process is invoked (GOSUB bbb).

3. After the game has been completed, the IF statement on line 30 tests the variable E1 (the "end of program" variable, which must be set to zero during the Program.Begin routine or this won't work). If the end of program flag is false (=0), then the program will branch back to line 20 and call the game subroutine again. This process will be repeated until the E1 variable changes from false to true (IF E1=0 THEN 20).

4. When the variable E1 changes to a non-zero value, the test in the IF statement will no longer be true. The program will not branch back to statement 20, but will instead fall through to execute the call in line 40, which is the Program.End routine (GOSUB ccc).

5. When the end of program routine has been completed, the program will execute the END statement at line 50 and will stop execution. Our program will have come to a successful conclusion.

Since the natural flow of execution will stop at line 50, all statements numbered higher than 50 can only be executed as a portion of a subroutine. Beginning with line 60, we will define the subroutines referenced in the root section of the code. Any one of the three subroutines which we have referenced so far, the Program.Begin, Game, or Program.End subroutines may be defined first. We Have found it easier to code the "trunk" of the program first, so that the first subroutine we Will define will be the Game subroutine.

```
57 REM **********************
58 REM     GAME ROUTINE
59 REM GAME.BEGIN
60 GOSUB ddd
69 REM TURN (1,T)
70 GOSUB eee
80 IF E2=0 THEN 70
89 REM GAME.END
90 GOSUB fff
100 RETURN
```

Figure 15.3: Game Routine

With the Game process now defined, we may now go back to statement 20 and replace the "bbb" in the subroutine call with the number 60. Notice that the structure of the Game process is quite similar to the structure of the Program level structure. At this level, the computer will execute the Game.Begin subroutine, then execute the Turn subroutine until the variable E1 is not zero, and then will execute the Game.End subroutine. The RETURN statment will return control of the program back up to the level immediately above this one, so that the next statement executed after the RETURN at 100 will be the IF statement of line 20.

```
107 REM ********************
108 REM     TURN ROUTINE
109 REM TURN.BEGIN
110 GOSUB ...
119 REM PLAYER'S TURN
120 P=1 : GOSUB ...
129 REM COMPUTER'S TURN
130 P=2 : GOSUB ...
139 REM TURN.END
140 GOSUB ...
150 RETURN
```

Figure 15.4: Turn Process

The Turn level is the next to be defined, and it will look a bit different from the first two levels. Instead of a repetitive subroutine at the player level, we will have two explicit calls, one for each player (the human and the computer). We will set a flag before each call so that we may use a common subroutine to award player pieces.

Again, we replace the unknown subroutine location in line 70 with the number 110. (The ":" in the code above allows one to put multiple statements on a single line)

Now that the trunk of the program structure is defined, we can begin to define the "branches" of the tree. First, we'll develop the Program.Begin process.

```
158 REM *******************
159 REM PROGRAM.BEGIN ROUTINE
160 DIM N$(15),A(2,6),T(2)
170 PRINT "THE GAME OF BUG"
180 PRINT " "
190 INPUT "ENTER YOUR FIRST NAME ",N$
200 PRINT N$;", DO YOU KNOW HOW TO PLAY THE GAME OF BUG?"
210 INPUT "ANSWER (Y OR N) ",X1$
220 E1=0
230 IF X1$(1,1) "Y" THEN GOSUB ...
240 RETURN

248 REM ********************
249 REM EXPLANATION OF RULES
250 PRINT "IN THE GAME OF BUG, EACH PLAYER TAKES A TURN"
260 PRINT "ROLLING A DIE. EACH NUMBER OF THE DIE CORRESPONDS"
270 PRINT "TO A PIECE OF A BUG'S BODY: 1=BODY, 2=NECK, 3=HEAD"
280 PRINT "4=ANTENNA, 5=TAIL, AND 6=LEG. YOU NEED ONE BODY,"
290 PRINT "1 NECK, 1 HEAD, 2 ANTENNAE, 1 TAIL, AND 6 LEGS TO"
300 PRINT "COMPLETE A BUG. ALSO, YOU MUST HAVE A BODY BEFORE"
310 PRINT "YOU CAN RECEIVE A NECK, LEGS, OR A TAIL; YOU MUST"
320 PRINT "HAVE A NECK BEFORE YOU CAN RECEIVE A HEAD, AND YOU"
330 PRINT "MUST HAVE A HEAD BEFORE YOU CAN RECEIVE ANTENNAE."
340 INPUT "HIT RETURN TO START THE GAME ",X1$
350 RETURN
```

Figure 15.5: The Program.Begin Routines

The remainder of the program is developed in like fashion, with subroutines developed according to the program design structure. The completed program is shown in its entirety in the listing of which follows.

```
  7 REM ********************
  8 REM    BUG PROGRAM
  9 REM PROGRAM.BEGIN
 10 GOSUB 160
 19 REM GAME (1,G)
 20 GOSUB 60
 30 IF E1=0 THEN 20
 39 REM PROGRAM.END
 40 GOSUB 610
 50 END

 57 REM ********************
 58 REM    GAME ROUTINE
 59 REM GAME.BEGIN
 60 GOSUB 360
 69 REM TURN (1,T)
 70 GOSUB 110
 80 IF E2=0 THEN 70
 89 REM GAME.END
 90 GOSUB 530
100 RETURN

107 REM ********************
108 REM    TURN ROUTINE
109 REM TURN.BEGIN
110 GOSUB 430
119 REM PLAYER'S TURN
120 P=1 : GOSUB 640
129 REM COMPUTER'S TURN
130 P=2 : GOSUB 640
139 REM TURN.END
140 GOSUB 450
150 RETURN

158 REM ********************
159 REM PROGRAM.BEGIN ROUTINE
160 DIM N$(15),A(2,6),T(2)
170 PRINT "THE GAME OF BUG"
180 PRINT " "
190 INPUT "ENTER YOUR FIRST NAME ",N$
200 PRINT N$;", DO YOU KNOW HOW TO PLAY THE GAME OF BUG?"
210 INPUT "ANSWER Y OR N ",X1$
220 E1=0
230 IF X1$ "Y" THEN GOSUB 250
240 RETURN
```

```
248 REM ********************
249 REM EXPLANATION OF RULES
250 PRINT "IN THE GAME OF BUG, EACH PLAYER TAKES A TURN"
260 PRINT "ROLLING A DIE. EACH NUMBER OF THE DIE CORRESPONDS"
270 PRINT "TO A PIECE OF A BUG'S BODY: 1=BODY, 2=NECK, 3=HEAD"
280 PRINT "4=ANTENNA, 5=TAIL, AND 6=LEG. YOU NEED 1 BODY,"
290 PRINT "1 NECK, 1 HEAD, 2 ANTENNAE, 1 TAIL, AND 6 LEGS TO"
300 PRINT "COMPLETE A BUG. ALSO, YOU MUST HAVE A BODY BEFORE"
310 PRINT "YOU CAN RECEIVE A NECK, LEGS, OR A TAIL; YOU MUST"
320 PRINT "HAVE A NECK BEFORE YOU CAN RECEIVE A HEAD, AND YOU"
330 PRINT "MUST HAVE A HEAD BEFORE YOU CAN RECEIVE ANTENNAE."
340 INPUT "HIT  RETURN  TO START THE GAME ",X1$
350 RETURN

357 REM ********************
358 REM GAME.BEGIN ROUTINE
359 REM CLEAR THE BUG ARRAY
360 FOR I=1 TO 2
370 FOR J=1 TO 6
380 A(I,J)=0
390 NEXT J
400 NEXT I
410 E2=0
420 RETURN

428 REM ********************
429 REM TURN.BEGIN ROUTINE
430 INPUT "HIT  RETURN  TO START YOUR TURN ",X1$
440 RETURN

448 REM ********************
449 REM  TURN.END ROUTINE
450 T(1)=0 : T(2)=0
460 FOR I=1 TO 2
470 FOR J=1 TO 6
480 T(I)=T(I)+A(I,J)
490 NEXT J
500 NEXT I
510 IF T(1)=12 THEN E2=1 ELSE IF T(2)=12 THEN E2=1
520 RETURN

528 REM ********************
529 REM  GAME.END ROUTINE
530 IF T(1)=12 THEN GOSUB 570 ELSE IF T(2)=12 THEN GOSUB 590
540 INPUT "WOULD YOU LIKE TO PLAY ANOTHER GAME? ",X1$
550 IF X1$ "Y" THEN E1=1
560 RETURN

568 REM ********************
569 REM PLAYER WINS MESSAGE
570 PRINT "CONGRATULATIONS ";N$;" YOU BEAT ME!"
580 RETURN
```

```
588 REM ********************
589 REM COMPUTER WINS MESSAGE
590 PRINT "HA, I WON. COMPUTERS PLAY BETTER THAN HUMANS"
600 RETURN

608 REM ********************
609 REM PROGRAM.END ROUTINE
610 PRINT "THANKS FOR PLAYING. TRY AGAIN SOME OTHER TIME"
620 PRINT "BYE."
630 RETURN

636 REM ********************
637 REM    TURN ROUTINE
638 REM TURN.BEGIN
639 REM  ROLL THE DIE
640 R=INT((RND(0)*6)+1)
650 IF P=1 THEN PRINT N$;"'S ROLL IS A ";R
660 IF P=2 THEN PRINT "COMPUTER'S ROLL IS A ";R
670 IF R=1 THEN GOSUB 790 ELSE 690
680 GOTO 780
690 IF R=2 THEN GOSUB 850 ELSE 710
700 GOTO 780
710 IF R=3 THEN GOSUB 930 ELSE 730
720 GOTO 780
730 IF R=4 THEN GOSUB 1010 ELSE 750
740 GOTO 780
750 IF R=5 THEN GOSUB 1090 ELSE 770
760 GOTO 780
770 IF R=6 THEN GOSUB 1170
780 RETURN

788 REM ********************
789 REM  ROLL = 1 ROUTINE
790 IF A(P,1)=0 THEN GOSUB 810
800 RETURN

808 REM ********************
809 REM AWARD PLAYER A BODY
810 A(P,1)=1
820 IF P=1 THEN PRINT N$;" GETS A BODY"
830 IF P=2 THEN PRINT "COMPUTER GETS A BODY"
840 RETURN

847 REM ********************
848 REM  ROLL = 2 ROUTINE
849 REM IF PLAYER HAS A BODY THEN CONTINUE
850 IF A(P,1)=1 THEN GOSUB 870
860 RETURN

867 REM ********************
868 REM ROLL = 2 CONTINUED
869 REM IF PLAYER HAS NO NECK THEN GIVE HIM ONE
870 IF A(P,2)=0 THEN GOSUB 890
880 RETURN
```

```
888 REM ********************
889 REM AWARD PLAYER A NECK
890 A(P,2)=1
900 IF P=1 THEN PRINT N$;" GETS A NECK"
910 IF P=2 THEN PRINT "COMPUTER GETS A NECK"
920 RETURN

927 REM ********************
928 REM  ROLL = 3 ROUTINE
929 REM IF PLAYER HAS A NECK THEN CONTINUE
930 IF A(P,2)=1 THEN GOSUB 950
940 RETURN

947 REM ********************
948 REM ROLL = 3 CONTINUED
949 REM IF PLAYER HAS NO HEAD THEN GIVE HIM ONE
950 IF A(P,3)=0 THEN GOSUB 970
960 RETURN

968 REM ********************
969 REM AWARD PLAYER A HEAD
970 A(P,3)=1
980 IF P=1 THEN PRINT N$;" GETS A HEAD"
990 IF P=2 THEN PRINT "COMPUTER GETS A HEAD"
1000 RETURN

1007 REM ********************
1008 REM  ROLL = 4 ROUTINE
1009 REM IF PLAYER HAS A HEAD THEN CONTINUE
1010 IF A(P,3)=1 THEN GOSUB 1030
1020 RETURN

1027 REM ********************
1028 REM ROLL= 4 CONTINUED
1029 REM IF PLAYER HAS LESS THAN TWO ANTENNAE THEN GIVE HIM ONE
1030 IF A(P,4) 2 THEN GOSUB 1050
1040 RETURN

1048 REM ********************
1049 REM AWARD PLAYER AN ANTENNAE
1050 A(P,4)=A(P,4)+1
1060 IF P=1 THEN PRINT N$" GETS AN ANTENNA"
1070 IF P=2 THEN PRINT "COMPUTER GETS AN ANTENNA"
1080 RETURN

1087 REM ********************
1088 REM  ROLL = 5 ROUTINE
1089 REM IF PLAYER HAS A BODY THEN CONTINUE
1090 IF A(P,1)=1 THEN GOSUB 1110
1100 RETURN

1107 REM ********************
1108 REM ROLL = 5 CONTINUED
1109 REM IF PLAYER HAS NO TAIL THEN GIVE HIM ONE
1110 IF A(P,5)=0 THEN GOSUB 1130
1120 RETURN
```

## The Savings Account Report Program

The savings account report program is developed in the same way as was the BUG program. However, we shall not develop it in complete detail. There are two reasons for this. First, this program requires that we do some fairly extensive formatting of the print lines, so that the columns of figures will line up correctly. Unfortunately, this is a cumbersome process in most versions of BASIC. For many versions of the language this requires the use of the PRINT USING statement, which, for the purposes of this book, does much to detract from the understandability of the structuring process. Also, this program uses an input file, something that many smaller systems without mass storage devices cannot handle. Therefore, the exact process for reading records into the computer is not given; it varies so much from one machine to the next that any one version of the implementation is of little value. Each individual will have to write a "read record" subroutine for this program which will handle all of the appropriate code for reading records.

```
1128 REM ********************
1129 REM AWARD PLAYER A TAIL
1130 A(P,5)=1
1140 IF P=1 THEN PRINT N$;" GETS A TAIL"
1150 IF P=2 THEN PRINT "COMPUTER GETS A TAIL"
1160 RETURN

1167 REM ********************
1168 REM  ROLL = 6 ROUTINE
1169 REM IF PLAYER HAS A BODY THEN CONTINUE
1170 IF A(P,1)=1 THEN GOSUB 1190
1180 RETURN

1187 REM ********************
1188 REM ROLL = 6 CONTINUED
1189 REM IF PLAYER HAS LESS THAN SIX LEGS THEN GIVE HIM ONE
1190 IF A(P,6) 6 THEN GOSUB 1210
1200 RETURN

1208 REM ********************
1209 REM AWARD PLAYER A LEG
1210 A(P,6)=A(P,6)+1
1220 IF P=1 THEN PRINT N$;" GETS A LEG"
1230 IF P=2 THEN PRINT "COMPUTER GETS A LEG"
1240 RETURN
==========================================================
```

```
  7 REM ******************************
  8 REM SAVINGS ACCOUNT REPORT PROGRAM
  9 REM PROGRAM.BEGIN
 10 GOSUB 840
 19 REM YEAR
 20 GOSUB 50
 29 REM PROGRAM.END
 30 GOSUB 300
 40 END

 47 REM ********************
 48 REM   YEAR ROUTINE
 49 REM BEGIN.YEAR
 50 GOSUB 800
 59 REM ACCOUNT (1,A)
 60 GOSUB 100
 70 IF E1=0 THEN 60
 79 REM YEAR.END
 80 GOSUB 340
 90 RETURN

 97 REM ********************
 98 REM  ACCOUNT ROUTINE
 99 REM ACCOUNT.BEGIN
100 GOSUB 730
109 REM MONTH (1,M)
110 GOSUB 150
120 IF E2=0 THEN 110
129 REM ACCOUNT.END
130 GOSUB 360
140 RETURN

147 REM ********************
148 REM   MONTH ROUTINE
149 REM MONTH.BEGIN
150 GOSUB 670
159 REM DAY (1,D)
160 GOSUB 200
170 IF E3=0 THEN 160
179 REM MONTH.END
180 GOSUB 430
190 RETURN

197 REM ********************
198 REM   DAY ROUTINE
199 REM DAY.BEGIN
200 GOSUB 630
209 REM TRANSACTION (1,T)
210 GOSUB 250
220 IF E4=0 THEN 210
229 REM DAY.END
230 GOSUB 490
240 RETURN
```

```
247 REM ********************
248 REM TRANSACTION ROUTINE
249 REM DEPOSIT (0,1)
250 IF T$="D" THEN GOSUB 600
259 REM WITHDRAWAL (0,1)
260 IF T$="W" THEN GOSUB 570
269 REM ADJUSTMENT (0,1)
270 IF T$="A" THEN GOSUB 540
279 REM TRANSACTION.END
280 GOSUB 510
290 RETURN

297 REM ********************
298 REM PROGRAM.END ROUTINE
299 REM CLOSE TRANSACTION FILE
300 CLOSE (0,Z0)
309 REM CLOSE ACCOUNT BALANCE FILE
310 CLOSE (1,Z1)
319 REM CLOSE YEAR END DATE FILE
320 CLOSE (2,Z2)
330 RETURN

338 REM ********************
339 REM  YEAR.END ROUTINE
340 PRINT "TOTALS FOR ";Y0$;Y1;Y2;Y3
350 RETURN

357 REM ********************
358 REM ACCOUNT.END ROUTINE
359 REM ACCOUNT CURRENT BALANCE = MONTHLY CURRENT BALANCE
360 A3=M3
370 PRINT "TOTAL FOR ACCOUNT ";A0$;A1;A2;A3
379 REM ADD ACCOUNT CREDIT AMOUNT TO YEARLY CREDIT AMOUNT
380 Y1=Y1+A1
389 REM ADD ACCOUNT DEBIT AMOUNT TO YEARLY DEBIT AMOUNT
390 Y2=Y2+A2
399 REM ADD ACCOUNT CURRENT BALANCE TO YEARLY CURRENT BALANCE
400 Y3=Y3+A3
409 REM TEST FOR YEAR END (END OF FILE)
410 IF Z0=1 THEN E1=1
420 RETURN

427 REM ********************
428 REM MONTH.END ROUTINE
429 REM MONTHLY BALANCE, BALANCE FWD = DAILY CURRENT BALANCE
430 M3=D3 : B5=D3
440 PRINT "FOR THE MONTH OF ";M0$;M1;M2;M3
449 REM ADD MONTHLY CREDIT AMOUNT TO ACCOUNT CREDIT AMOUNT
450 A1=A1+M1
459 REM ADD MONTHLY DEBIT AMOUNT TO ACCOUNT DEBIT AMOUNT
460 A2=A2+M2
469 REM TEST FOR END OF ACCOUNT
470 IF A0$ A$ THEN E2=1
480 RETURN
```

```
487 REM ********************
488 REM  DAY.END ROUTINE
489 REM TEST FOR END OF MONTH
490 IF M0$ M$ THEN E3=1
500 RETURN

507 REM ********************
508 REM TRANSACTION.END ROUTINE
509 REM GET NEXT RECORD
510 GOSUB aaa
519 REM TEST FOR END OF DAY E4
520 IF D0$ D$ THEN E4=1
530 RETURN

537 REM ********************
538 REM ADJUSTMENT ROUTINE
539 REM ADD ADJUSTMENT AMOUNT TO DAILY BALANCE
540 D3=D3+A9
550 PRINT "ADJUSTMENT ";A9;D3
560 RETURN

567 REM ********************
568 REM WITHDRAWAL ROUTINE
569 REM SUBTRACT DEBIT AMOUNT FROM DAILY BALANCE
570 D3=D3-A9
580 PRINT "WITHDRAWAL ";A9;D3
590 RETURN

597 REM ********************
598 REM  DEPOSIT ROUTINE
599 REM ADD DEPOSIT AMOUNT TO DAILY BALANCE
600 D3=D3+A9
610 PRINT "DEPOSIT ";A9;D3
620 RETURN

627 REM ********************
628 REM DAY.BEGIN ROUTINE
629 REM PRINT DAY NUMBER
630 PRINT D$;
639 REM INITIALIZE OLD DAY FIELD
640 D0$=D$
649 REM INITIALIZE END OF DAY FLAG
650 E4=0
660 RETURN

667 REM ********************
668 REM MONTH.BEGIN ROUTINE
669 REM INITIALIZE MONTHLY TOTALS
670 M1=0 : M2=0 : M3=0
679 REM PRINT MONTHLY HEADING
680 PRINT M$;"ACTIVITY";"BALANCE FORWARD OF";B5
690 PRINT "DATE ACTION DR CR BALANCE"
699 REM INITIALIZE OLD MONTH FIELD
700 M0$=M$
709 REM INITIALIZE END OF MONTH FLAG
```

```
710 E3=0
720 RETURN

727 REM ******************
728 REM ACCOUNT.BEGIN ROUTINE
729 REM INITIALIZE ACCOUNT TOTALS
730 A1=0 : A2=0
739 REM PRINT ACCOUNT HEADINGS
740 PRINT "ACCOUNT#";A$
749 REM GET ACCOUNT BALANCE FORWARD
750 GOSUB bbb
759 REM INITIALIZE BEGINNING MONTHLY BALANCE FORWARD
760 B5=A5
769 REM INITIALIZE OLD ACCOUNT FIELD
770 A0$=A$
779 REM INITIALIZE END OF ACCOUNT FLAG
780 E2=0
790 RETURN

797 REM ********************
798 REM YEAR.BEGIN ROUTINE
799 REM INITIALIZE YEARLY TOTALS
800 Y1=0 : Y2=0 : Y3=0
809 REM PRINT YEARLY HEADING
810 PRINT Y9$
819 REM INITALIZE END OF YEAR FLAG
820 E1=0
830 RETURN

838 REM ********************
839 REM PROGRAM.BEGIN ROUTINE
840 PRINT "SAVINGS ACCOUNT REPORT"
850 PRINT "FOR THE YEAR ENDED";
859 REM OPEN FILES
860 GOSUB ccc
869 REM GET YEAR END DATE
870 GOSUB ddd
879 REM READ FIRST TRASACTION RECORD
880 GOSUB aaa
890 RETURN

aaa REM READ TRANSACTION RECORD
    This subroutine will read the next transaction record.

bbb REM READ ACCOUNT BALANCE FORWARD
    This subroutine will read the account balance forward record.

ccc REM OPEN FILES
    This subroutine will open all program files.

ddd REM READ YEAR ENDED DATE
    This subroutine will get the year ended date record.
```

# 16

# Afterword

## Self-Documenting Code

Working in the area of structured design education, we are often confronted with the argument: "I don't need a structured software design methodology. I am currently programming in one of the high level languages, and all of my code is structured and self-documenting. Why is it necessary to add an extra, unneeded layer of program documentation in the form of a logical program design when my program already does exactly the same thing?"

This is an important issue which needs to be addressed. Many people feel that if, indeed, a program is self-documenting and written in a high level structured language, then there is no need for a logical program design--the code itself will suffice as documentation. This is an argument (often an emotional one) which on the surface seems quite sound, but it has some real problems. In reality, there is a great deal of justification for doing a logical program design before such code is written. The reasons for that will be explored in this chapter.

## Structured Design Techniques

An underlying concept in all of the structured design techniques is the separation of the program design from the program construction. To use an analogy with computer hardware, these techniques stress the separation of the "program schematic" if you will, from the "program circuit board." This is a fairly new and quite important concept to understand.

Before any program construction can be done, there must be some sort of program design, where the goals and objectives of the program are stated and the construction guidelines are drawn up. This is no different from the computer hardware construction techniques; a schematic diagram is drawn up and verified before any wiring of components is considered.

This separation of "logical design" from "physical design" is an important one--one that we can exploit in program design techniques to gain us a number of distinct advantages. A single logical schematic diagram, for instance, can be physically implemented in a number of different ways, depending on the physical characteristics required of the finished component. The physical implementation will be different if the circuit is required to respond in one nanosecond or one microsecond; it will be different if the circuit is required to operate between 0 and 30 C or between -50 and 150 C. But in both of these instances, the logical design will remain the same.

The same feature is true of logical software designs; they can be physically implemented in a number of different ways depending on the hardware restrictions or the output requirements. A logical on-line inquiry system may be implemented one way if is going to be required to work on a tape-driven system; it may be implemented quite differently on a disk-driven system. But the logical program design is still the same.

## Superprogrammers

The structured revolution never really had any effect on the excellent programmers that were around. Nor was it probably meant to. Even before the so-called "structured" techniques made their appearance, all of the really good computer programmers did some sort of a rudimentary program design before they wrote any code--even if it was all done in a split second in their head and nothing was ever written down. These programmers never needed any kind of structuring devices; it was all very natural and intuitive to them to produce running programs. Of course, they themselves were never quite sure of the process by which they arrived at a working program, so their abilities were never transferable; they couldn't teach the rest of us how to do what they did.

Unfortunately, the "superprogrammers" of the world are few and far between, and the commercial data processing industry cannot depend on them to do all of the work--there is simply too much to do. In the same way, they cannot be expected to do all of the work in the microcomputer industry either. The bulk of the software work that must be done will be completed by ordinary people with no particular talent for creating programs. And most of us non-superprogrammers need some sort of method to collect and organize our thoughts before we attempt to put together a program; to us the process of producing a correct and working program is not intuitive and natural.

There is a definite need to be able to teach the non-superprogrammers of the commercial DP industry and the new people working with the microcomputers how to program correctly.

## Design Techniques

We have already mentioned that it is important to separate the logical portion of the program design from the physical portion. But if we move a step back from even that, we see two other processes which must be delineated in a production environment: design must be a separate and distinct phase from construction.

This splitting of design and construction is not a new or novel idea; it has been in use in engineering for hundreds of years. It is the application of these ideas to the task of program production that is new and warrants some discussion.

The actual program construction today is no big deal; structured programming seems to be the way to go. Contrary to popular belief, there is no such thing as an unstructured programming language. It is possible and desirable to do structured programming in any language in existence. Granted, some languages lend themselves to structuring more easily than others, and in some of the languages you have to allow for the use of the GOTO, but in our experience we have seen people do very nicely structured work in most any language you can name: RPG, Assembler, FORTRAN, APL, etc. Thus, no matter what facilities you have available, you can implement logical program designs in a consistent and structured fashion.

When you look at the design portion of the process, you can find all sorts of nice boxes and diagrams floating around. There are the Warnier-Orr Diagrams, Bubble Charts, Nassi-Schniederman or Chapin Charts, Flowcharts, HIPO Diagrams, Structured Design Language (SDL), etc. The important thing to realize about these things is that they are all simply tools to aid us in our design efforts. They help us organize our thoughts and collect them in a consistent manner. Using any one of them will produce better results than using nothing at all.

However, just like the programming languages, there are some tools which are easier to use than others. The Bubble Charts and the Nassi-Schniederman/Chapin Charts are helpful at the high end of a design, and not very useful for doing detail work. The HIPO

Diagrams are useful at all levels, but they tend to be cumbersome and wordy. The Flowcharts and SDL are also helpful at all levels, but they are often difficult to read and therefore understand.

The Warnier-Orr diagram has emerged from this group of tools as the premier design and documentation device. Warnier-Orr diagrams are easy to read and understand, and lend themselves nicely to design at all levels, from the very abstract and indefinite to the very concrete and detailed. They seem to be the best design tools that we have available today.

## The Importance of Design

Many people feel that program design is a waste of valuable programmer time and effort. This is true not just of the programmers who are forced to do the designs. Many managers exhibit definite symptoms of the WISC (Why Isn't Sammy Coding) Syndrome. Some DP managers seem to feel that any programmer time not spent coding is wasted time and not to be tolerated.

This is an attitude which needs to be changed. The fruits of doing program production in the manner outined above are demonstrable and readily apparent to the people who take the time to look for it.

We face some special problems with the microcomputer people in this area of recognizing the importance of design. First of all, most microcomputer applications tend to be relatively small ones, and the chances of success without a measurable design phase are fairly good. This is no different than the carpenter who can put together a simple shed without a plan, or the electronics hobbiest who can put together a flashlight without a schematic diagram. But on large applications, this likelihood of success becomes much smaller, and we end up with large, cumbersome, and often incorrect systems.

No one ever starts out to write an unstructured program; they become that way by degrees. A small change here, a patch there, a program fix there, and before you know it, your small, readable system has become a large unstructured, unreadable monster program that is harder than ever to adjust or fix. These systems are the reason that the cliche has sprung up that large systems are never completely debugged; for every bug that is fixed two more will turn up that are even harder to fix.

This problem of debugging was one that lingered on in the commercial DP industry for a long, long time. For many years, the solution was thought to be better debugging techniques. But the bugs are only the manifestation of a much larger problem: the lack of a coherent design to begin with. There are hundreds of organizations throughout the world today whose debugging problems have all but vanished. They are writing programs that run the first time, simply because they took the time to design a solution to their problem before they created a program.

## Creativity

Another reason that the microcomputer people are so wary of the structured design techniques is that the techniques lack creativity. There is little room for "personalized code"; all structured programs look pretty much like all of the other structured programs. It is only within the unstructured code that you begin to find a great deal of variety.

This is perhaps the most valid of the arguments against doing structured design and/or programming in the microcomputer area. The hobbiests feel hamstrung by the rigidity of the design techniques, and they want to be able to program creatively. This is quite alright, as long as the program is never going to be used by anyone else. This is the same argument that you will find from real APL affectionados: their language is like a game. The game is to see if you can find a way to compress an entire program down into a single line of code. Now, as an intellectual exercise or as a piece of true artwork, this is quite fine. But as a technique for producing application software that is going to be maintained and adapted, this is totally unacceptable.

It has been often pointed out that such "cute" programs are all but totally worthless as far as production programs are concerned; when they have to be changed usually they have to be done over. This mistake was one which the commercial DP industry recognized and eliminated; the microcomputer people would do well not to repeat this mistake.

## Flexibility and Adaptability

There are a couple of overriding advantages to doing software development in this structured fashion. One of the advantages has already been mentioned: the techniques allow people to write programs that run correctly the first time and virtually eliminate debugging. This advantage would probably be a justification for using the techniques in and of itself. But there is another: the flexibility and adaptability that you gain from doing a logical design.

This flexibility is one that will particularly help the microcomputer software industry. With the many different machines available today and the many different languages which they program in, having a logical software design is a tremendous advantage. Adapting the same logical design to run on many different types of machines is no longer a cumbersome and difficult task. In fact, it is a simple process of translation, and we are already hearing of instances where people are generating code by computer from a logical software design. This says something significant about the process of adaptation: it is very simple and easy to do.

## Conclusion

The arguments against structured design and structured programming being heard in the microcomputer industry today are roughly similar to the arguments against the structured techniques heard a few years ago in the big, commercial data processing shops. Many of the commercial shops have tried the techniques and found that they work. In fact, some of the most satified people using the techniques today are the skeptics who said "This won't work, and I'll do a project with them just to prove you wrong." They did their project, and found out that all that had been said about the advantages of structured design were true.

It has come to the point now that we can begin to teach people to produce superprograms without becoming superprogrammers, and as more and more people are called upon to be familiar with some type of computer and to program it in some way, this skill needs to be more and more transferable. The structured design techniques provide that skill.

# Bibliography


Constantine, L. and E. Yourdon, Structured Design. New York: Yourdon Inc., 1975.

Dahl, O., E. Dijkstra, and C. Hoare, Structured Programming. New York: Academic Press.

Higgins, David A., "Structured Program Design," BYTE Magazine, October, 1977.

_______, "Structured Programming with Warnier-Orr Diagrams," BYTE Magazine, December 1977, January 1978.

Jackson, M. A. Principles Of Program Design. New York: Academic Press, 1975.

Orr, K.T., Structured Systems Development. New York: Yourdon Press, 1977.

Warnier, J. D., Logical Construction of Programs. New York: Van Nostrand Reinhold Co., 1976.